Vorwort

„Media For You“ wendet sich an Auszubildende in den Berufen *Kaufleute für audiovisuelle Medien, Medienkaufleute Digital und Print Kaufleute für Marketingkommunikation* und *Veranstaltungskaufleute*. Die neuen und neu geordneten lernfeldorientierten Bildungsgänge sehen mindestens 40 Jahreswochenstunden Unterricht in der Fremdsprache vor.

Zur Benutzung des Buches

Konzeption

Die Kapitel sind jeweils unterteilt in einen allgemeinen Teil und vier berufsbezogene Module, die sich auf die oben genannten Berufe beziehen. Sie sind durch unterschiedliche Modulnamen und Raster gekennzeichnet:

AV-Medien – Kaufleute für audiovisuelle Medien (audiovisual media)
Verlag – Medienkaufleute Digital und Print (publishing)
Marketing – Kaufleute für Marketingkommunikation (advertising)
Event – Veranstaltungskaufleute (event)

Die berufsbezogenen Module sollen dabei helfen, die im allgemeinen Teil erworbenen Kenntnisse und Fertigkeiten mit dem entsprechenden Fachbezug und -vokabular zu vertiefen. Darüber hinaus erleichtern sie die Integration des Faches Englisch in bildungsgangspezifische Lernsituationen und stellen somit einen Bezug zu den Lernfeldern der Ausbildungsberufe her.

Icons

Zur Erleichterung der Benutzung befinden sich neben den *tasks* folgende Icons:

Hörtext im Audio-Portal
Partnerarbeit bzw. Rollenspiel
Gruppenarbeit bzw. Projekt

Aufgaben ohne Icon sind schriftlich und in Einzelarbeit zu lösen.

Begleitmaterialien

Dieses Buch wird durch eine CD-ROM für Lehrkräfte sowie durch Hörtexte ergänzt, die im Audio-Portal zum Download unter www.bildungsverlag1.de/audio-Portal zur Verfügung stehen. Die **CD-ROM** für Lehrkräfte enthält neben Lösungsvorschlägen für alle Übungen auch weiterführende Materialien, wie z. B. zusätzliche Übungen und *activities*. Außerdem enthält sie zu jedem Kapitel einen Aufgabenteil mit KMK-Prüfungsaufgaben, die zur Vorbereitung auf das **KMK-Fremdsprachenzertifikat** dienen. Das Zertifikat bescheinigt ein fremdsprachliches Handlungsprofil, das sich an den Erfordernissen des Berufsfelds orientiert. Dabei wird von den Kompetenzbereichen Rezeption, Produktion, Mediation und Interaktion ausgegangen.

Weitere Informationen zum KMK-Fremdsprachenzertifikat finden sich auf der Homepage der Kultusministerkonferenz (http://www.kmk.org/fileadmin/veroeffentlichungen_beschluesse/1998/1998_11_20-RV-Fremdsprachen-berufliche-Bildung_02.pdf) und bei den Schulministerien der Bundesländer

Die Autoren

Inhaltsverzeichnis

My Company

1

Kick-off: Introducing people

Aims

You learn
... how to introduce yourself or a colleague
... how to make small talk
... how to talk about your job, the company, and its products

Task 1

Listen to the dialogues.
Listen again and make a list of useful expressions, e. g.:
Pleased to meet you. My name is ...
Nice to meet you. I am ...
How do you do.
Good morning. How are you?
Fine, thanks, and you?
Nice to see you again.

Task 2

Work with a partner. Find out the following facts about him or her.

- Name
- Address
- School
- Company
- Occupation
- Hobbies

Task 3

Work with a group. Introduce your partner to the group.

1 Unit

Expression Bank

- May I introduce …? He/She works in … for … as a …
- This is … He/She went to school in … and left school in …
- He/She lives in … His/Her hobbies are …
- Please meet … He/She works as a …

Task 4

Work with a partner. Translate the following questions into English, and answer each question correctly for yourself.

a) *Was machen Sie beruflich?*

b) *Wie ist das Wetter heute?*

c) *Welches war Ihr Lieblingsfach in der Schule?*

d) *Treiben Sie viel Sport?*

e) *Reisen Sie viel?*

f) *Welche Art von Büchern/Filmen/Musik mögen Sie?*

g) *In welchem Unternehmen arbeiten Sie?*

Info Point

When you meet an English-speaking person, do not just give your family name, like people often do in Germany. Always give both your first and last name. It sounds more friendly to say 'Hello, my name is Anne Krüger' than just to say "Krüger", and it is easier to understand. English-speaking people tend to use first names in conversation right from the start.

Topics

Topic 1: The formal organisation of media companies

The formal organisation

A media company needs a structure in order to achieve its objectives. The formation of a structure begins at an early stage of its development as a result of the need to group different activities.

- Activities are separated into departments such as acquisition, marketing, finance, production, and personnel. Further subdivisions will develop as the organisation grows in size.
- Tasks are divided in such a way as to make use of specialist technical and management skills.
- Relationships between employees are defined.
- Rules and procedures to be followed are established.
- It is established where decisions are to be made.
- Channels of communication are created through which information and decisions may pass.

The formal organisation structure may best be represented by an organisation chart (see below). The diagram indicates a number of features of organisational structures:

- The grouping of activities on the basis of functions.
- The division of labour: The degree of specialisation and technical skills is indicated, both between and within departments.
- The chain of command: The lines of control and responsibility are clearly shown. The broken lines show where a department has specialist functional responsibility throughout the organisation.
- The communication channels: Unbroken lines show formal lines of communication within the organisation. What is not shown are the horizontal and diagonal communication channels which develop either formally or informally within the organisation.

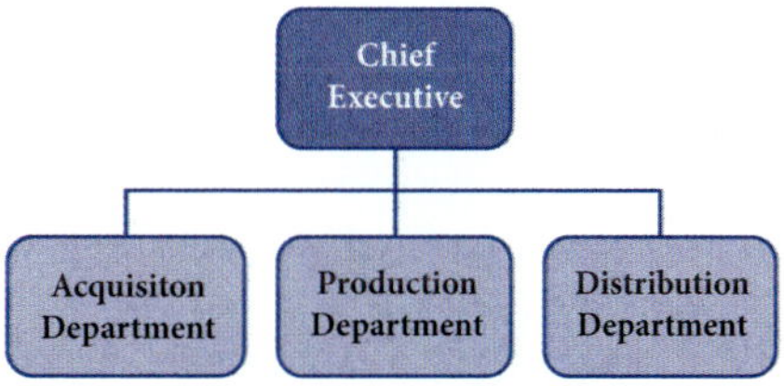

Simple structure of a media business organisation

Task

Work with a partner. Draw the structure of your company. You can use the words you will find in the particular word list that is related to your job.

Unit 1

Topic 2: Talking about your job

My job

Task 1

Read the description of Anne Krüger's job and answer the questions below.

My name is Anne Krüger. I am a trainee and I work for Schiller GmbH, a publishing house in Cologne which publishes a daily local newspaper and several magazines. Currently, I work in the distribution department. We supply 250,000 subscribers and five wholesale traders with our daily newspaper. My main task is to deal with our subscribers in Cologne. For example, I am responsible for deliveries to subscribers in certain areas of Cologne. When a subscriber complains that he has not received his copy of the local newspaper, I have to contact the delivery service and prepare all the necessary documents.
I like my job because it is interesting. One has to be able to work with people, and to make decisions. It is important to listen to customer complaints and get the job done at the right time so that the subscriber gets his daily newspaper in the nick of time. If everything goes well, the subscriber is satisfied and keeps on subscribing to our paper. However, if the newspaper is not delivered to the customer's satisfaction, we may lose a subscriber.
My typical working day is hard to describe because I do not do the same things every day. There are often problems which I have got to solve, but my job is never boring. However, I spend many hours sitting at my desk, so I really need to do sport in my leisure time. I go to the gym at least twice a week, and in summer I play tennis whenever I have the time. A lot of my friends play badminton, but I do not like it. Most days I get up at 6:30 am and have breakfast before I leave the house at about 7:30 am. I usually go to work by tram, and on the way I read a book. When I get home in the evening I am usually too tired to go out.
I am not working in the office twice a week, because I am attending vocational school on Mondays and Fridays. It is quite hard work because there are a lot of details to learn. As a kind of reward, I have the Friday afternoons off.
In the course of my training, I will be transferred to the advertising department next month.

Task 2

Work with a partner. Ask questions about Anne and use these question words: what – who – where – which – why – how – when

Task 3

Find the English equivalents for the following expressions:

a) *Wir beliefern …*

b) *Man muss Entscheidungen treffen können.*

c) *Ich verbringe viele Stunden am Schreibtisch.*

d) *Abonnenten*

e) *Am Freitag Nachmittag habe ich frei.*

Task 4

Describe your own job and a typical day in your working life. Use expressions from Anne's statement. You may also use the table below as a help.

I work for … as …	(company, job)
Our main branches are in …	(cities)
The company was founded in …	(year)
We employ …	(no. of employees)
The persons I am in most frequent contact with are …	(job titles, not names)
Our main departments are …	(e. g. accounts department)
Our main goods/services are …	
Our most important suppliers are …	(line of business, not names)
Our main customers are …	(line of business, not names)
Our major competitors are …	
My main task is to …	
A typical day …	

Task 5

Work with a partner. Ask and answer questions about each other's job. Ask each other about present activities and current short-term projects, courses and so on.

Task 6

Office relationships and responsibility: Insert these words in the text below.

words, words, words

employee	employer	staff
colleague	superior	subordinate
direct superior	head of department	CEO (chief executive officer)
director	manager (2)	co-worker
officemate	supervisor	report to
responsible for	in charge of	

If you work in a company, you are its ________________ and a part of its ________________. The people you work with are your ________________ or ________________. If you share an office with them, they are your ________________.
The ________________ is the company you work for and is led by the ________________, the head of the company.
The person whom you ________________ is your boss. Anyone who is above you in the organisational structure is your ________________; your boss is your ________________. The word ________________ is rather used for someone who observes and directs your work, as in a factory. Anyone below you in the company is your ________________ (however, this term is not often used as it sounds arrogant).
Someone who is ________________ or ________________ a whole department is called ________________.
A ________________ is usually responsible for a whole area of a company, whereas a ________________ can be responsible for just one or several products or projects (e. g. a product or project ________________).

Info Point

The words *chef* or *chief* must not be confused with the German word *Chef.* A *chef* is a cook and a *chief* is either the leader of an Indian tribe or an American police officer. However, *chief* can be used as an adjective in order to denominate superiority such as in *chief accountant*, i.e. the main accountant among several accountants.

Jobs in the film and music business

Task 1

Match the jobs below with their correct description.

Film – electric:	**Film – camera:**
a) *grip*	k) *director of photography*
b) *gaffer*	l) *camera operator*
c) *best boy*	
Film – production:	**Music:**
d) *production assistant*	m) *A&R representative*
e) *assistant director*	n) *recording engineer*
f) *casting director*	o) *sideman*
g) *location scout*	p) *publisher*
h) *location manager*	q) *producer*
i) *script/continuity*	r) *band/personal manager*
j) *set dresser*	

1. The technical specialist(s) in charge of setting-up and operating recording gear during a recording session. They spend much of their time at the mixing board, but they are also responsible for operating, adjusting, and even repairing other recording equipment, including microphones, cables, and multitrack recorders. They collaborate closely with producers to bring the artistic vision of a song or album into recorded reality.
2. He/She assists the director of a movie long before the shooting starts. Of greatest importance are the breakdowns, which are created by going through the script several times, each time pulling out different information and organising it by scene number. That way the shooting schedule is created.
3. He/She negotiates prices for shooting locations, gets permits and insurance to make sure the filming is legal, and organises the logistics so that filming can take place without obstacles.
4. The person responsible for developing an artist's career. He/She typically advises the artist on all business decisions and attempts to promote the artist through all available means, including demos, media coverage, and person-to-person networking.
5. The artistic director who oversees the creation of an album or other musical recordings. Like the director of a movie, he/she is ultimately responsible for the overall artistic success of a recording. In major label recordings, the artistic skills of this person are often more important than those of the artist, particularly in more electronically generated genres such as rap, hip-hop, and dance music.

6. They make sure the shots of a film match. Since a film is not shot in sequence, several days or weeks may pass between two subsequent scenes. Now it is their job to see that the hair, make-up, and costumes all match in those two scenes.
7. The role is technical, creative and administrative: they supervise set-up and operation of production equipment, help plan programme format, and research scripts, maintain production records and hire equipment. Unlike other roles in the industry, they are more generalist than specialist and are involved in all stages of the production process.
8. Being a … has nothing to do with your personality or sex. After several jobs as a lighting technician, possibly serving under many different gaffers, you will get called up out of the ranks to become a …
9. A professional musician who is hired to perform or record with a group of musicians of which he is not formally a member. This term is often used interchangeably with *session musician*.
10. Their job is to make stars – more specifically, to give actors work. They have to invite actors for a prereading and choose the ones best suited for the film. The final decision, however, is made together with the director and the producer.
11. They file for registration of copyrights, issue licenses, and collect royalties on behalf of the copyright owner of a song, usually the author(s). By long-standing industry tradition, the author and the … each typically collect 50% of the royalty income.
12. This misleading job title is just simply the head of the lighting crew. He/She also hires the lighting technicians.
13. If the entire film is going to be filmed on a stage, then there is no need for this job. Most films, though, have at least one exterior location, and as long as there is one, you need someone to find the *right* one.
14. The person who actually sits behind the camera and looks through the lens.
15. They make the scene look authentic – if the film plays in the 60s, it is their job to find the right background decoration, e. g. Beatles posters instead of Backstreet Boys on a teenager's bedroom wall.
16. He/She works together closely with the director of a film because they are the ones who really design the colour, the feel and the mood of a film. He/She instructs the lighting technicians and the camera operators.
17. These people are the "muscle" of the film set. Whenever an item on set needs to be hidden or moved – they will be there for you. A special form is the dolly … – he/she lays out the dolly tracks and pushes the dolly (manual camera vehicle).
18. They are the staff at record labels responsible for scouting new artists and then (to some extent) helping develop those artists after a recording contract has been signed. The phrase is left over from early in the music industry when the A&R position involved selecting both the musicians (artists) and the music (repertoire) for any given recording.

Task 2

Find out about British and American media companies.
Search the internet and find out about the following things:

a) *What major TV stations (public and private) are there in the USA and GB?*

b) *Pick one station (e. g. the BBC or CNN) and find out about its structural organisation – which departments are there, which jobs can you exercise there?*

c) *Find out about major and independent music labels in the USA and GB – are they the same, which kind of music do they publish, which of them can also be found in Germany?*

Jobs in the publishing business

Task 1

Read the following text and answer the questions in written form.

Multimedia Pub is a multimedia publisher dedicated to the delivery of information to professionals, combined wherever possible with smart information tools. Multimedia Pub is a global operator with a prolific history, a prosperous present and a promising future. Multimedia Pub is one of the most important information providers in the health, corporate & financial services, tax, accounting, legal, regulatory, and education markets.

Who we are

Multimedia Pub is a multinational information services company with revenues of EUR 3.4 billion and listed on Euronext in Amsterdam (Euronext 100 index). Multimedia Pub has long been known as a publishing company, but we are much more than that. Today we are an allround provider of content, software and services, delivering in all formats that our customers require. With our 20,000 employees, we serve professional customers in the fields of health, corporate & financial services, tax, accounting, legal, regulatory, and education.

Known throughout the world as the leading content provider, we are strengthening our position as a full product and service provider to professionals around the globe. Our ambition is to be 'the essential knowledge company' for our customers.

What we do

Historically, Multimedia Pub was a traditional publisher with a focus on print products. Thanks to a transformation on all levels, our operations are now more market-driven than ever, offering a choice of advanced electronic products and services as well as print. We sell information, software and services, often on a subscription basis. We do this in many different formats via the medium that best suits the customer, varying from Internet-related products and CD-ROMs to books, professional journals and loose-leaf publications. We offer solution-oriented, smart information tools that help our customers improve their productivity and the quality of their work.

Our customers

The worldwide activities of Multimedia Pub are aimed at a select target group: professional customers. By professional customers we mean experts, such as:

- pharmaceutical companies and pharmacists
- medical specialists and nurses
- banking, insurance and securities professionals
- accountants, lawyers and fiscal experts
- teachers, students and educational institutions

All Multimedia Pub businesses are closely committed to their customers and markets. There is a direct connection between the added value of our products and the success of our customers. The relationship with our customers is therefore built on partnership and co-operation, so that we can deliver the right information, at the right time, via the right medium.

Three aspects are crucial here: our products and services must excel in quality, accessibility and userfriendliness. That is why our ambition is to be 'the essential knowledge company' for our customers.

A global presence

Alongside our corporate office in Amsterdam, the Netherlands, we have a presence in more than 25 countries. Our companies are located in Europe, North America, Australia and Asia serving customers worldwide.

Multimedia Pub's activities are organised around five core market groups. This structure not only reflects the breadth of our customer base but also promotes synergy within the group. It enables us to benefit from the wealth of expertise available within Multimedia Pub as well as the economies of scale of a worldwide enterprise like ours.

1. In your own words, how does a publishing company like Multimedia Pub present itself?
2. Describe the five core market groups of Multimedia Pub.
3. Work out the most important company figures.

Task 2

Write a short report on a typical working day.

Task 3

Summarise the following text in your own words.

Multimedia Pub is in the business of providing high quality content products and smart information tools for professionals. Multimedia Pub is a leading player in the fields of health, corporate & financial services, tax, accounting, legal, regulatory, and education.

Empowering talents

Everything we do, and all of our decisions, center around this fundamental mandate. The products and services we provide and the processes we develop to facilitate sustained growth focus on the customer. The smart information tools we deliver enable professionals to become more productive as they use their considerable talents to find solutions for some of the most pressing issues of today.

Knowledge sharing

A company's worth is defined by two elements: people and knowledge. We have a professional commitment to creating and selling integrated systems and services for our clients and their people. We make sure clients can distribute information and share knowledge. With smart information tools, we help professionals achieve new levels of productivity and efficiency.

Jobs in the advertising business

Advertising account executive
Reporting to the account manager, executives act as a link between client and agency. They have overall responsibility for the smooth running of campaigns in their care and deal with the day-to-day turnaround of work, ensuring it is produced on time and on budget. Executives put the proposal together and set up meetings to present the brief and estimate costs to the client. They inform the client at every stage and ensure they are happy with the work as it progresses.

Art director
Advertising art directors work on the 'visual' side of advertising. Working as part of a creative team, they work closely with writers to create original ideas using a brief from the client. Their role is to interpret what the client wants to say in an interesting way. They are also responsible for engaging other members of the team, such as illustrators, photographers, designers or Mac operators in the project. The director will oversee the work from the initial concepts, until completion of the finished product.

Copywriter
Copywriters work in a creative partnership with an art director to conceive, develop and produce effective advertisements. While the art director deals mainly with the visual images, it is the copywriter who provides the verbal or written aspect. This involves writing 'copy', i.e. coming up with the original catch phrases, slogans and straplines.

Media analyst
Within a media organisation, a media analyst acts as an information and research expert for both agency staff and external clients.
The role involves preparing detailed media evaluation reports and taking responsibility for finding the answers to specific research questions that would lead to more effective marketing campaigns. Media analysts run qualitative and quantitative research, and use general research skills to carry out their role.

Media buyer
Media buyers communicate on behalf of their clients with media sales companies in order to purchase the most appropriate advertising space within a range of media including digital, radio, press, television and the Internet. Employed by media companies and advertising agencies, their role involves a high level of negotiation over the phone for the most cost-efficient and effective advertising space. The job also involves frequent contact with clients. Media buyers may work across a range of media or specialise in one particular area. In some companies, the role and function of media buying is combined with that of media planning.

Media planner
Media planners enable their clients to maximise the impact of their advertising campaigns through the use of a range of media. In order to ensure that campaigns reach their target audiences as effectively as possible, media planners combine creative thinking with factual analysis to develop appropriate strategies. They apply knowledge of media and communication platforms to identify the most appropriate vehicle for building awareness of a client's brand.

Marketing executive

Marketing executives in this field are involved in promoting and selling fast-moving consumer goods (FMCGs) and products to the public, usually via the retail trade. FMCGs are typically high-volume, low-value items with high public visibility and short life span, such as food, drink, confectionery, toiletries, and household goods.

Marketing executives work on various projects to support the brand/marketing manager in developing brands and promoting existing products, raising public awareness of the client's products through advertising campaigns and in-store promotions and building brand loyalty.

Task

Answer the following questions.

a) *Which of these positions are represented in your own company/agency? Describe one of the jobs in more detail by providing examples from your own company/agency.*

b) *Which of these people do you have the most frequent contact with – describe your relation to him/her.*

c) *In which of these positions would you like to work in the future? Make a list of things that you like about the job.*

d) *Judging from your own experience – which requirements are there for these jobs?*

So, you want to be an event manager?

Event management involves planning, organising and managing small, medium and large scale operations at a variety of venues such as football stadiums, entertainment centres, parks and multi-purpose complexes. Events could be a local fun run, a community event like the George Street Festival in Brisbane, an exhibition or a world class sporting competition like Formula One or even the Olympic Games.

Event managers are responsible for overseeing all aspects of an event to make it successful and enjoyable for everyone involved. In order to achieve this you will be required to work cooperatively with sponsors, the media, participants and volunteers.

You will be responsible for preparing budgets, promoting the event through sponsorship, advertising, media coverage, liaising with the local community, coordinating signage, ticketing, parking and catering – just to name a few! You'll

also be responsible for the strategic development of the event if it is to be held more than once and prepare business plans to ensure its future success.
To be an event manager, you'll need well developed communication skills. You'll also need to be able to work autonomously and as part of a team with strong leadership and decision-making skills.

Gina Kay (29) – event manager at Carrots event agency – on a day in her working life

"As event manager I am mainly responsible for the management of all kinds of events for our clients. This could be anything from incentive travel, meetings and conferences to weddings and any kind of party, for example. There is an incredible variety of tasks related to this and therefore every day is different and the job never gets boring. A typical day could start with the planning of an event by putting together an offer and a budget plan. This may be followed by negotiating a contract with a different client. Usually, the phone starts ringing at about 9am. There is a lot of correspondence to be initiated and responded to regarding different aspects of one event or dealing with different events at the same time. This also includes coordinating tasks and colleagues. Of course you definitely have to like to deal with different people all the time and to face all kinds of problems. Additionally you must not be afraid of long hours and stressful situations as there is often some pressure when an event is due to take place. My working week may well have 40 to 70 hours. In order to succeed in this line of work you need to be hard working, independently or as part of a team, be a good communicator, be motivated and responsible and have good attention to detail as well as having the overall view of one or several events and all the tasks and people involved at the same time."

Task 1

Get together in groups according to the kind of company you work for, e. g. fair trade, booking agency, catering service.

a) *Prepare a small presentation of such a company regarding its structure and your typical working day.*

b) *Present the company and your working day in front of class.*

Info Point

If you have problems preparing a presentation, have a look at unit 5 on meetings (page 99) and the corresponding skill file (page 143). There you find information on how to structure a presentation and on how to communicate your information.

Variety of events

Working in the event industry involves developing and planning many different kinds of events. Below you find different areas of service such as *meeting planning, special events, destination management, corporate sponsorship* – each with a case study of a corresponding event. The case studies all originate from the American event agency Event Logistics, Inc.

Meeting planning

A Fortune 500 telecommunications company chose Event Logistics, Inc. to coordinate their International Technical Symposium at Walt Disney World in Orlando. The program would include the participation of the company's top executives from all over the world and culminate in a gala event.
Event Logistics managed all aspects of the program including:

- Site research and selection
- Development of online registration process
- Management of worldwide registration data
- Hotel negotiations
- Arrangement of hotel accommodation for all participants
- Management of all onsite logistical needs associated with the corporate meetings
- Creation of special closing event at MGM Studios

Special events

Event Logistics, Inc. was selected to create the 100th anniversary celebration for a Fortune 500, international retail and manufacturing corporation. The history-making event was to be held on one day, and encompass four different activities and venues – a press conference, an employee business meeting, a cocktail dinner and a celebration show.
Hundreds of details needed to be coordinated, including:

- Invitations
- Database management for the 2,000 guests invited to the celebration
- A staffed, dedicated "event line" to coordinate responses
- The design and production of museum-quality graphics displays
- Arrangements for the use of more than a dozen collector vehicles and tires
- Catering and decorations
- Talent procurement of varying music genres
- Coordination of hotel and travel arrangements for guests from all across the U.S. plus ten foreign countries.
- Ground transportation to and from all four events

Destination management

Event Logistics, Inc. was asked to create and execute a corporate incentive for the top sales producers of a national Fortune 50 retail and manufacturing corporation.

Event management duties included:

- Site research and selection
- Hotel negotiations
- Invitations
- Staffing an "event line" to coordinate responses
- Coordination of all travel arrangements
- Hotel accommodation and airport meet and greet services
- Onsite meeting management
- Creation of special award dinner and various evening events
- Schedule day tours – everything from helicopter trips to submarine rides
- Arranged for celebrity race car drivers to make guest appearances at events
- Incorporate company mascot into each of the week-long events
- Transportation (air and ground)

Corporate sponsorship

A publicly traded financial services company commissioned Event Logistics, Inc. to develop and implement a national charity event sponsored by the company. Known as 18 Wheels of Hope, the year-long program was designed to recruit members of the trucking industry to donate truckloads of food to a nationally known charity and then join together in Dallas for a campaign celebration and truck parade.

Serving as "programme headquarters," Event Logistics coordinated all aspects of the event including:

- Staffing an "event line" to coordinate national participant registration, media inquiries and food donation efforts
- Liaison between corporate sponsor, benefiting charity and trucking industry members
- Comprehensive public relations involving national news and trucking industry media
- Production of all programmes, press and collateral materials
- Development of incentive programmes throughout the year to encourage trucking industry involvement
- Coordination of a parade through downtown Dallas, for a convoy of 100 trucks
- Arrangement of nationwide drop-points for food donations
- Production and placement of select advertisements in trade publications
- Creation of a special "awards" event at Texas Stadium to honor those involved in the charity effort

Source: Event Logistics, Case Studies, 2006, www.eventlogistics.com/case.study/index.html, [15.08.2011]

Task 2

Pick an event you are or have been involved in.

a) *Prepare a small case study of it similar to the ones by Event Logistics. Pay attention not to publish any confidential data.*

b) *Present the case study in class.*

Correspondence in the media business

2

Kick-off: Understanding and writing business letters

Task

Discuss your experience in class:

In the office …
- … how often do you read catalogues, papers or business letters?
- … how often do you write letters in English?
- … do you find it difficult to read or write letters in English?
- … do you normally communicate in English to native or non-native speakers of English?

Aims

You learn …
… how to identify the elements of a business letter
… how to communicate via letter or e-mail
… how to ask for information about products or services
… how to order products or services
… how to make a complaint if things do not go as planned

Topics

Topic 1: Elements of business letters

In modern business communication it is vital that information is exchanged quickly and effectively. So, when writing business letters you should follow certain conventions.

A **Neptune & Shoreditch Limited**

194 Ebury Street
London
B SW1 8UP

C Ms J. Redding
Advertising Department D
Newspaper Group Limited E
3 Canada Square
Canary Wharf
London
E 14 5DT

F August 14, 2012

Dear Ms Redding G

Reference number AD 265 H

I Thank you for your fax of today, in which you informed us that the printing material for our advertisement has not yet arrived at your office.

J I have looked into this, and indeed, the printing material has not left our marketing department yet, due to an unforeseen shortage of staff during the summer period. I have already entrusted one of my staff to deliver the printing material personally at short notice.

I would like to apologise for the inconvenience you have suffered and to thank you for your patience.

K I look forward to receiving your confirmation of the safe arrival of the printing material and to doing further business with you.

Yours sincerely L

Louisa Fox M

Louisa Fox N

Head of Marketing Department O

Task 1

Identify the letter parts and match them.

1. body (of the letter)
2. complimentary close
3. date
4. opening
5. ending
6. signature
7. recipient's company
8. recipient's address
9. salutation
10. sender's position
11. sender's address
12. postcode
13. sender's name
14. subject line
15. recipient's name

Elements of business correspondence

British vs. American form

Im Folgenden werden nur die regional abweichenden Varianten berücksichtigt. Alle übrigen Bestandteile eines Geschäftsbriefes werden separat aufgeführt.

	 **UK**	 **USA**	Internationally accepted:
Date	9/5/20__ (day/month/year)	5/9/20__ (month/ day/year)	20__-05-09 (year-month-day)
Inside address (recipient address)	Mr James Brown 6 Brook Street Ealing London W53 4AU UK Remember: Messrs, Mrs, Ms, Miss or Mr are written in the same line as the name. The post code is written below the place name.	Greg Gatto 1435 Silk Avenue Santa Barbara, CA 45489 USA Remember: In the USA they are often left out completely. The zip code is written on the same line after the place name, separated by a comma.	

	UK	USA	Internationally accepted:
Companies as legal entities	'Limited' or 'Ltd', 'PLC' or 'plc' after the names of British companies	'Inc' or 'Corp.' after the names of American companies	
Salutation and complimentary close	Dear Sir or Madam, Dear Sir/Madam, Dear Sirs **corresponds with** Yours sincerely, Yours faithfully --------------------- Dear Miss Miller **corresponds with** Yours sincerely, Kind regards, Best regards --------------------- Dear Customer **corresponds with** Yours sincerely --------------------- Dear Sarah **corresponds with** Best regards, Kind regards, Best wishes	(Ladies and) Gentlemen: **corresponds with** Sincerely, Very truly yours --------------------- Dear Madam Chairperson: **corresponds with** Very truly yours, Sincerely --------------------- To whom it may concern: **corresponds with** Sincerely --------------------- Dear Ms White: **corresponds with** Sincerely, Cordially, Yours truly --------------------- Dear Peter: **corresponds with** Regards, Cordially	
Punctuation with salutation and complimentary close	The **standard** or the **open** form can be applied: **Standard:** Dear Mr. Miller, Yours sincerely, **Open:** Dear Mr Miller Yours sincerely	The **closed** form is applied: Dear Mr. Miller: Sincerely,	

Unit 2

	UK	USA	Internationally accepted:
Subject line	Dear Mr Wright Your letter of July 6, 2012 We are sorry to …	Your letter of July 6, 2012 Dear Mr Wright: We are sorry to …	The subject line may be underlined, typed in CAPITAL LETTERS or **bold type** Some companies write "Subject:" or "Re" in front of the subject line. Remember: In English the first word of the body of the letter starts with a capital letter.

Task 2

Use the letter on page 25 as example and rewrite this letter using the correct spacing and punctuation.

Neville Jackson Designers & Manufactures of Exclusive Fitted Furniture Broadway Business Park Ashburton Road West Trafford Park Manchester M17 1RW Sept 12, 2012 Ms J Redding Advertising Department Newspaper Group Limited 3 Canada Square Canary Wharf London E 14 5DT Dear Joanne Our advertisement in last week's Magazine I am writing about our advertisement that was published in your Magazine last week When I examined the printing quality I found that it was not up to the sample you received prior to printing As evidence I am enclosing another sample I think that the damage was caused by the loss of our sample We would ask you to compensate us for the poor quality by granting us a discount of 15 % I trust that you will settle the matter speedily and to our satisfaction Yours sincerely Ross Mitchell Marketing Department Enclosure.

Communication via e-mail

Info Point

Business letters are often replaced by communication via e-mail with a tendency to be less formal. Yet the writer of good e-mails may not lack a number of skills such as software knowledge, time management and a good command of language. Though e-mails often seem to be spontaneous, they require some consideration about what is to be said and to whom they are directed. Using software anyway, the writer is advised to use a spell-checker before sending the e-mail.

A request for the current rates card of *The Times* may look like this:

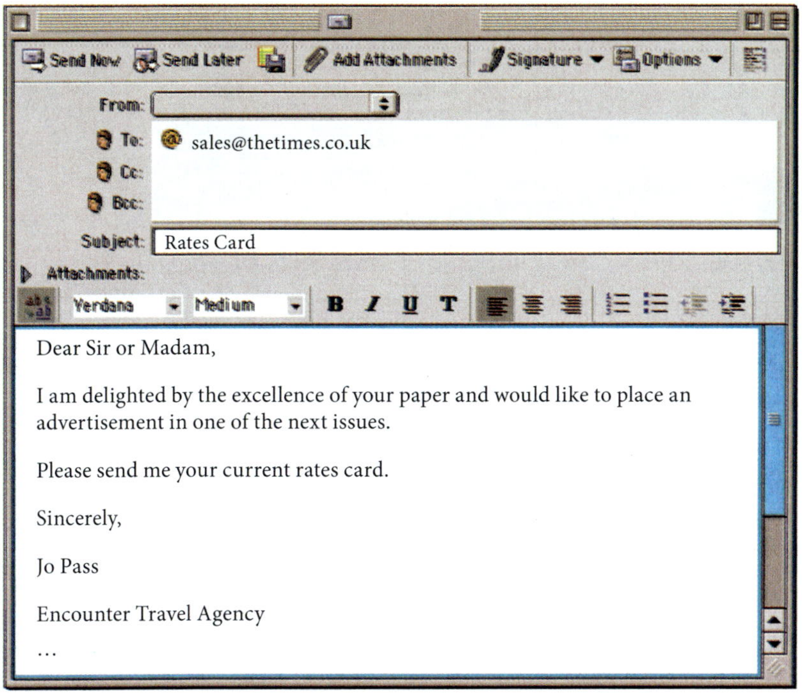

From:
To: sales@thetimes.co.uk
Cc:
Bcc:
Subject: Rates Card
Attachments:

Dear Sir or Madam,

I am delighted by the excellence of your paper and would like to place an advertisement in one of the next issues.

Please send me your current rates card.

Sincerely,

Jo Pass

Encounter Travel Agency

...

A less formal approach:

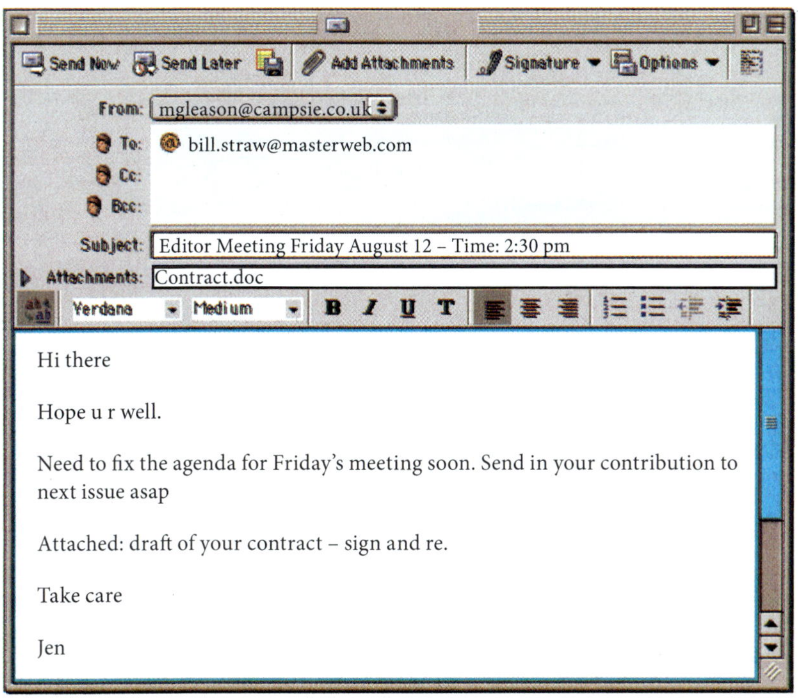

From: mgleason@campsie.co.uk
To: bill.straw@masterweb.com
Cc:
Bcc:
Subject: Editor Meeting Friday August 12 – Time: 2:30 pm
Attachments: Contract.doc

Hi there

Hope u r well.

Need to fix the agenda for Friday's meeting soon. Send in your contribution to next issue asap

Attached: draft of your contract – sign and re.

Take care

Jen

Informal e-mails tend to use abbreviations, contractions and short forms; names are given as first names only and/or as nick names. Of course, one rule applies to all e-mails: be polite, try to avoid commands (e. g. "Send me the requested item immediately").

Task 3

Make a contrasting list of formal and informal elements in e-mails and compare.

formal elements	informal elements
Dear Sir or Madam	Hi (there)
...	...

Info Point

Short forms are often found in e-mails, such as

asap	as soon as possible
BR	best regards
CC	carbon copy (a copy of the e-mail to somebody else)
BCC	blind carbon copy (copy to a third person without the addressee's knowledge)
Ta, Thanx	Thank you
r	are
u	you
ICU	I see you
FYI	for your information

Task 4

Check the Internet for more abbreviations.

Topic 2: Enquiries

Gathering information about certain offers, products or services is an important part of modern business relationships. If you would like to compare the prices of different suppliers for instance, it is necessary to write an enquiry.

Info Point

There are two kinds of enquiries: *general* or *specific*. A *general enquiry* can be just a request for information about a product or a service, a quotation or an estimate. If you ask for more detailed information, you will write a *specific enquiry*.

An enquiry about a catalogue (American structure):

Ken Beam
2520 Crete Avenue
Olympia, WA 98501

Johnson Brothers
3487 23rd Street
New York, NY 12009

Dear Sir or Madam: September 12, 2012

With reference to your advertisement in yesterday's New York Times, could you please send me a copy of your latest catalogue. I would also like to know if it is possible to make purchases online.

Yours faithfully

Ken Beam

Ken Beam
Managing Director
English Learners Inc.

Phrases, Phrases, Phrases: Enquiry

Expression Bank

- **The start:** Dear Sir or Madam, Dear Mr/Mrs/Ms/Miss ...
  To Whom It May Concern – (very formal as you do not know the person to whom you are writing)
- **Giving reference:** With reference to your advertisement (ad) in . . .
  Regarding your advertisement (ad) in . . .
- **Requesting a catalogue, brochure, etc.:** After the reference, add a comma and continue – . . . , would (could) you please send me . . .
- **Requesting further information:** I would also like to know . . .
  Could you tell me whether . . .
- **Signature:** Yours faithfully – (very formal as you do not know the person to whom you are writing)

Task 1

Writing an enquiry

Last weekend you attended a home & garden exhibition in Kew Gardens, London. You were interested to see an English company which had garden sheds on display. Write to Garden Shed plc, 260 Woodham Lane, New Haw, Addlestone, Surrey, KT15 3NS, refer to the exhibition and ask for a brochure of the latest models.

Task 2

Writing enquiries from German prompts

Situation:
Sie arbeiten für den Buchverlag Bell Medi@ GmbH, Hugo-Eckener-Straße 1, 50829 Köln, und interessieren sich für Produkte der British Library.

Ihre Aufgabe:
Entwerfen Sie eine Anfrage an die British Library, auf deren Internetseite Sie beim Surfen gestoßen sind. Ihr besonderes Interesse gilt den Ausstellungskatalogen der letzten beiden Jahre. Sie interessieren sich für den Vertrieb der Kataloge in deutschsprachigen Ländern, da Sie als Kunstverlag schon viele diesbezügliche Anfragen hatten. Sie bitten um genaue Daten und um Angabe von Preisen für Wiederverkäufer. Fragen Sie nach Lieferbedingungen und Lieferfristen. Stellen Sie in Aussicht, dass Sie auch, falls der Vertrieb erfolgreich wird, am Erwerb einer Lizenz für die deutschsprachigen Ausgaben interessiert sind. Geben Sie der Hoffnung Ausdruck, bald von der British Library zu hören.

Words, words, words

book publisher – Buchverlag
exhibition catalogue – Ausstellungskatalog
distribution – Vertieb
German speaking countries – deutschsprachige Länder
art publisher – Kunstverlag
resaler – Wiederverkäufer
acquisition – Erwerb
licence – Lizenz

Info Point

Addresses in Great Britain have a postcode (e. g. KT15 3NS) whereas addresses in the United States have a ZIP code (e. g. CA 45678).

Topic 3: Offers

If a potential client addresses an enquiry to you, you need to be able to respond in an appropriate way in order to establish a business relationship.

Info Point

Entering into a business can be expressed by an offer in oral or written form. Two kinds of offers can be found: The *solicited offer* (an answer to a customer's enquiry) and the *unsolicited* or *voluntary offer* (an offer which hasn't been asked for). An offer is legally binding unless the customer does not react within a reasonable period of time. The offer can be declared as *without engagement* or it can contain the phrase *subject to prior sale.*

An offer for notebooks

SpiceMedia, a distributor of rare films on DVD, operates internationally. There are offices all over Europe, and a lot of English speaking employees work for the international markets. Recently, there has been a need for replacing out-dated computers by new ones. Tamarics has been asked to submit an offer for notebook packages, i.e. notebooks with printers and software. Here is Tamarics' offer:

Tamarics Retail Ltd.
Maylands Avenue
Hemel Hempstead
Herts, HP2 7TG
England
e-mail: info@tamarics.co.uk

August 6, 2012

SpiceMedia
German Branch
Mathias-Brüggen-Straße 12
50827 Köln
Germany

Dear Herr Steinberg

Your enquiry of August 2, 2012

Thank you for your interest in our products and your enquiry of August 2, 2012

We are pleased to quote as follows:

10 Notebook Packages TASHIBA (HMS Processor 2.53 GHz, 2 MB Cache, 4 GB RAM, 500 GB hard drive, SuperMulti DVD ReWriter, WiFi wireless, 15" TFT display, GO Printer and business software pack) at £624.97 each, excluding VAT.

Our prices are quoted EXW Hemel Hempstead.

We do business on the basis of payment by irrevocable documentary letter of credit in our favour, payable at Forbes bank.

Shipment can be effected immediately on receipt of order.

Our offer is valid until September 1. We can offer 2 % cash discount for payment within 10 days. Please note that our products come with a three-year warranty.

Please do not hesitate to contact us if you have any further questions. We hope this quotation will meet your expectations and we look forward to hearing from you soon.

Sincerely
Tamarics Retail Ltd.

Jaswinder Singh

Jaswinder Singh
Export Manager

2 Unit

Expression Bank

- **The start:** Dear Sir or Madam, Dear Mr/Mrs/Ms/Mrs
  To whom it may concern – (very formal as you do not know the person to whom you are writing)
- **Thanking for an enquiry:** Many thanks for your enquiry **of** June 6, ... **about** our range of products; We were pleased to learn that you are interested in our …
- **Making an offer:** We would now like to give you/to submit/to make the following quotation: …
- **Stating terms of delivery and payment:** The prices are to be understood EXW Barnstaple/FOB Newcastle/FCA Cologne Airport; Our usual terms of payment are cash with order/cash against documents/40 days net, 8 days 3 %; We would request payment by banker's draft/cheque/bank transfer.
- **Referring to the time of delivery:** Delivery/Shipment will be made ex stock/ immediately on receipt of order/one week after receipt of order.
- **Stating the validity of the offer:** The offer is valid until …/Without engagement
- **Giving additional information:** We can offer a 15 % quantity discount for orders over 50 units/2 % introductory discount
- **Suggesting further contact:** Please do not hesitate to contact/call us if you have any further questions.
- **Creating goodwill (closing sentences):** We hope this offer will find your approval/ meet your requirements; We look forward to hearing from you soon.

Task 1

Rewrite the offer restoring the correct order of the scrambled elements.

Enclosed you will find our summer catalogue and price list quoting prices CIF London. We are sure you will find a ready sale for our products in England, as have other retailers throughout Europe and America, and we hope very much that we can reach agreement on the terms quoted.

Dear Mr Cape

Encs.

Mr Jon Cape
General Manager
G. Lincoln & Co. Ltd
Newell Street
Birmingham B3 3EL
UK

Thank you for your interest. We look forward to hearing from you soon.
We always deal on payment by sight draft, cash against documents. However, we would be prepared to review this once we have established a firm trading association with you.

RomaMedia S.p.A.
Via di Pietra Papa, 00146 Roma

We can confirm that there would certainly be no trouble in supplying you from our wide selection of electronic equipment.

Telefono : +39(0)6 769910
Telefax : +39(0)6 6815473
E-mail : RizzoA@RomaMedia.it

Yours sincerely

We were pleased to receive your enquiry, and to hear that you liked our range of public-address systems.

A. Rizzo

YourRef.: Aug 6, 2012
OurRef.: E/1220

We can offer you a discount, which would be 5 % off net prices for orders over £ 2 000.

A. Rizzo
Sales Director

Task 2

Writing offers from German prompts

Der German American Culture Club (Ansprechpartner: Bill Jenkins) mit Hauptsitz in 1515 Market Street, Philadelphia, PA 19102, USA, hat an Sie als Mitarbeiter der SpiceMedia (SpiceMedia GmbH, German Branch, Mathias-Brüggen-Straße 12, 50827 Köln) eine Anfrage gerichtet. Der Club möchte für seine 50 Clubhäuser, die über die ganzen Vereinigten Staaten verstreut sind, zentral die DVD-Sammlung „Deutsche Literatur im Film“ bei Ihnen bestellen. Bieten Sie die Kollektion zum Einzelpreis von EUR 99,00 an, zuzüglich Kosten für Verpackung und Versand. Sobald die Bestellung vorliegt, können Sie ab Lager liefern mit der Bedingung EXW. Falls der Club umgehend bezahlt, können Sie 2 % Nachlass auf den Gesamtpreis anbieten. Bieten Sie an, dass Sie für Rückfragen selbstverständlich zur Verfügung stehen. Geben Sie Ihrer Hoffnung Ausdruck, bald vom Club zu hören.

Words, words, words

main office – Hauptsitz
can be found – verstreut sein
packaging and postage – Verpackung und Versand
from stock – ab Lager
immediatly – umgehend
discount – Nachlass

Topic 4: Placing an order

If you have collected all the information you require, you would now like to make a purchase. When making an order it is important to include all necessary information so the supplier knows exactly what to deliver.

An order from Professor Oppenheimer:

May 23, 2012

Mr Joe Black,
Director
Second Hand Books
Seattle, WA 98795

Dear Mr Black:
Would you please send me the following used books via COD? According to your website, orders need to include the title, author, and publisher.

Title	Author	Publisher
"Driving Home"	Jim Crawford	Johnson and Co.
"Christmas Fun"	Maggy Smiley	Roothers
"Landscaping Myths"	Jane Olderson	Nature plc.

Thank you very much,
Phil Oppenheimer

Phil Oppenheimer,
Professor, OUS
PO/to

Expression Bank

- Would you please send ...
- According to your website/magazine/leaflet, ...
- COD (cash on delivery)

Info Point

The initials at the bottom of the letter indicate who the letter is from, followed by who typed the letter – for example: from Ken Beare typed by Ron Easton = KB/re

Task 1

Writing offers from German prompts

Situation:
Als Mitarbeiter/in der Werbeagentur West, Hugo-Eckener-Straße 1, 50829 Köln, erhalten Sie am 10. des Monats eine schriftliche Anfrage der Taurus Event plc, 1,

Alfred Road, Maidstone, Kent, MA12 7RQ, die sich für den heimischen Vertrieb von kleinen Stoffbären, die Ihre Agentur erfolgreich als Werbegeschenke anbietet, interessiert.

Ihre Aufgabe:
- Formulieren Sie ein Angebot.
- Beziehen Sie sich dabei auf die Anfrage vom 10. des Monats.
- Ihre Agentur vertreibt seit 15 Jahren erfolgreich Werbegeschenke.
- Sie fügen Preislisten und Kataloge dem Angebot bei.
- Sie erläutern Rabatte (10 % ab 100 Stück, 20 % ab 500 Stück).
- Sie erläutern die Lieferbedingungen (4 Wochen nach Auftragseingang).
- Sie erwarten eine Zahlung netto Kasse.
- Das Angebot gilt 6 Monate ab Datum des Briefes.
- Sie hoffen auf einen baldigen Auftrag.

Words, words, words

advertising agency – Werbeagentur
local distribution – heimischer Vertrieb
cuddly bear – Stoffbär
promotional gift, freebie – Werbegeschenk
item – Stück
receipt of order – Auftragseingang
net cash –netto Kasse

Task 2

Writing orders from German prompts

Situation:
Die Werbeagentur West, Hugo-Eckener-Straße 1, 50829 Köln, erhält am 27. des Monats ein schriftliches Angebot der Ursus Printing plc, 27, Brook Road, Dartford, Kent, DA 10 8 LN über den Druck von 5 000 Flyern.

Ihre Aufgabe:
- Schreiben Sie mit Datum vom 1. einen Auftrag.
- Bedanken Sie sich für das Angebot vom 25. des Monats.
- Bestellen Sie die 5 000 Flyer zur Lieferung an Ihre postalische Anschrift.
- Die Lieferung sollte spätestens drei Wochen nach Auftragseingang frachtfrei bei Ihnen eingetroffen sein.
- Bitten Sie um eine schriftliche Auftragsbestätigung und um Benachrichtigung, falls der Liefertermin nicht eingehalten werden kann.
- Erwähnen Sie, dass Ursus Printing mit weiteren Aufträgen rechnen kann, falls die Flyer termingerecht und qualitativ einwandfrei geliefert werden.

Words, words, words

to be shipped to – zur Lieferung
postal address – postalische Adresse
carriage paid – frachtfrei
on time – termingerecht
in immaculate quality – qualitativ einwandfrei

Topic 5: Complaints

If a mistake has been made while processing an order for example, it is necessary to deal with complaints. In these situations it is important to deal with a dissatisfied customer in a polite way.

A dissatisfied customer

HappyDrivers Co.
3489 Elm St.
Olympia, WA 98502

August 17, 2012

Robert Greene, Vice President
Document Printers
Salem, MA 34588

Dear Mr Greene:
As someone who has worked with your company for over five years, we were very disappointed to see the documents you printed for our latest HappyDrivers Co. publicity campaign.
According to our written agreement, we expected full color brochures with explanatory texts, but instead, we found that black and white photos had been included in the prepared brochures. I think you will agree that a communication problem exists.
We would like you to provide us with the promised color coverage, or provide us with a refund.

Yours truly,

Sean J. Miller

Sean J. Miller,
Director
SJM/lj

Expression Bank

- As someone who has worked with . . ., we were very disappointed to find/see/ have discovered ...
- As our written agreement stipulated, we expected ...
- I think you will agree that a communication problem exists. We would like you to ..., or provide us with a refund.

Task 1

Writing a complaint

You are employed at the Stolberger Tageblatt, Hammerwald 10–20, 52224 Stolberg, and you are asked to write a complaint to James Barlow Printers, Holme Lane, Scunthorpe, North Lincolnshire, DN16 3RF, for not delivering 2,500 copies of a diary you ordered four weeks ago. The delivery was due, as stated in a written confirmation, five days ago.

Task 2

Writing complaints from German prompts

Situation:
Als Mitarbeiter/in der Werbeagentur West, Hugo-Eckener-Straße 1, 50829 Köln, haben Sie am 1. des Monats bei der Ursus Printing plc, 27, Brook Road, Dartford, Kent, DA10 8LN die Lieferung von 5 000 Flyern bis zum 21. des Monats bestellt. Der Auftrag wurde wenige Tage später unter Anerkennung der Bedingungen schriftlich bestätigt. Bis heute (25.) ist die Lieferung noch nicht eingetroffen.

Ihre Aufgabe:
- Schreiben Sie eine Rüge bezüglich des Lieferverzugs.
- Nehmen Sie Bezug auf Ihren Auftrag vom 1. des Monats.
- Erinnern Sie an die Auftragsbestätigung.
- Sie sind bereit, die Lieferung bis zum 30. des Monats zu akzeptieren, allerdings mit einem Rabatt von 30 %.
- Beenden Sie den Brief höflich.

Words, words, words

acknowlegement – Anerkennung **complaint** – Rüge

Looking for the right location

The success of a film often relies on the location it is shot in. A film set in mediaeval times for example does only 'look right' if the producers make sure that the environment and the buildings look authentic.

Task 1

Enquiring for a filming permit

For the following exercise, please work in pairs!

Situation:
The company you work for (Greenlight TV GmbH, Hansaring 52, 50696 Köln) prepares the production of a film which is to be shot in Scotland. The location scout has already found various castles that are suitable for a scene that requires an old castle set in wild scenery. He asks you to write to the castle's owners and ask for a filming permit. Shooting should take place on the 4th and 5th of August.

Task:
Write an enquiry, exchange it with your partner and write two answers – a positive and a negative one. Then discuss the letters you have exchanged and correct each other's mistakes!

Note: You may invent any details you like concerning both the film project and the castle.

Task 2

Complaining and apologising

Have a look at the apology on this page, then answer the following questions:

1. What did Ms Grant complain about?
2. What does Greenlight TV offer in order to appease Ms Grant?
3. Write the complaint that preceded this apology.

Apology

Dear Ms Grant,

Damage caused by film team

We were extremely sorry to learn about the damage caused by our film team. Although we acted with the utmost care in the rooms of your castle, some minor carelessness seems to have lead to this regrettable circumstance. We do hope that the damage can be fixed without leaving traces.

Of course, we are insured against such unfortunate cases and would therefore suggest to inspect the damage with an expert of our insurance company. Please let us know which date would suit you, and we will see to the matter immediately.

Again, please accept our apologies and do not hesitate to call us if you have any further questions.

Yours sincerely

Robert Heitkamp
Location manager
Greenlight TV GmbH

Ordering office supplies

You are employed at "Meerfeld Verlags GmbH", Steinfurter Straße 27, 67808 Eisenberg, as manager of the production department. Your boss has left the following note on your desk. Write the order, composing a complete business letter.

Hallo Frau/Herr . . .,

bestellen Sie bitte noch heute zur kurzfristigen Lieferung 10 000 Bogen[1] maschinenglattes Papier[2], Bestellnummer MFP 2000 NC bei Paper & More plc, Sales Department, 280 Caxton Rd, Dartford, Kent DA 10 8 RQ mit der Bitte um Angabe des Liefertermins und schriftlicher Bestätigung unseres Auftrags. Ihr Ansprechpartner ist Ihr Geschäftsfreund Tom Waits. Beziehen Sie sich bei Ihrer Bestellung auf das Angebot von Paper & More vom 25. März 2012.

Danke und Gruß, B. Oss.

Correspondence in advertising agencies

For an advertising agency to be able to deliver its services, it has got to deal with a range of different suppliers. In what follows, you establish a business relationship with a provider of printing services.

Task 1

Do Task 1 in the "Event"-section on page 42. Then base the answers to tasks 2 to 5 on the correct letter.

Task 2

Your advertising agency has been asked to design the menu cards and commemorative brochure for Jenny's Office Break launch party described above.

Write a specific enquiry to ImPrint Ltd to get information about their prices and terms for printing 50 menu cards (b/w, A4, 200 g paper) and 200 commemorative brochures (4c, A5, 20 pages, 120 g paper).
The address: Sarah Wilson, ImPrint Ltd, 32 Ealing Rd, London W12 5DL

Task 3

On the basis of your enquiry, write the solicited offer you would receive by ImPrint Ltd as an answer.

[1] sheet
[2] machine finished paper

Task 4

By referring to their offer, place the order with them.

Task 5

The ordered brochures and cards have arrived. Unfortunately, there is a spelling mistake on the menu cards and instead of 200, only 180 brochures were delivered.

Write the corresponding letter of complaint which would be appropriate in such a situation.

Correspondence in event agencies

When planning a major event, you have got to take care of a lot of things. A crucial aspect of its organisation is the way in which you communicate with the companies contributing their services. In the following tasks you practise how to write the respective letters to make sure that the event you are planning will be a success.

Task 1

Arrange the following snippets in the correct order to produce a coherent business letter.

1. To celebrate our launch we would like to invite you to a party at our headquarters in London on Thursday, September 10 at 5 pm. You will have the opportunity to try some delicious meals from our new menu and Jenny Wales, the chain's founder, will be there herself to talk about her management philosophy and autograph copies of her bestseller, "Recipes for success". If you wish to attend the launch please complete and return the enclosed reply to us by August 30. Details about Jenny's Office Break are also enclosed together with our menu and price list.

2. *Gina Conrads*
3. Sincerely yours
4. August 15, 2012
5. Are your employees fit for work? Or do they decide on the fast food choice – a burger and a can of soda – in their lunch break? It's possible that they don't get the nourishment they need to contribute the best to your business. We know you care about the health of your staff, and we have the perfect solution to your needs.

6. Dear Ms Miller

7. Enc.

8. Staples Ltd
   Human Resources Dept
   32 Knightsbridge
   London SW4 3AU

9. We very much hope to see you at the launch party and look forward to serving you and your staff in the near future.

10. Invitation to the launch of Jenny's Office Break – The new generation of office catering

11. Our ref. GC / PR

12. Jenny's Office Break is a fast-growing chain of office catering providing wholesome, tasty meals and snacks. We offer them at fair prices and with an environment-friendly wrapping. Quality and freshness are our top priority. Therefore, we only use locally grown ingredients originating from organic farming methods.

13. Jenny's Office Break Catering Service
    24 Ash Grove
    Ealing
    London W52 6KL

14. Gina Conrads (Ms)
    Public Relations Manager

15. FAO: Ms Sarah Miller, Human Resources Manager

Task 2

Your company has been asked to organise the launch event for Jenny's Office Break described above.

Write a specific enquiry to Harrods Ltd. to find out whether their food hall would be available for the event.
The address:
Harrods Ltd, Knightsbridge, Peter Johnson (marketing assistant), 87-135 Brompton Road, London SW1X 7XL, phone: +44 2077301234, fax: +44 2075810470, e-mail: pjohn@harrods.co.uk

Task 3

For the event you contact Balloons Ltd, a supplier of decoration articles, to get information about "healthy" decoration products.

Write a specific enquiry for corresponding products.
The address:
Balloons Ltd, Sandra Clark (Sales assistant), 36 Oxford Street, London W1 2AC,
phone: +44 3888401222, fax: +44 3888401223,
e-mail: sclark@balloons.co.uk

Task 4

On the basis of your enquiry write the solicited offer you would receive by Balloons Ltd as an answer.

Task 5

By referring to their offer, place the order with them but alter the size and amount of one of the products offered.

Task 6

The ordered products have arrived. Unfortunately, some have the wrong colour and some are missing completely.

Write the corresponding letter of complaint which would be appropriate in such a situation.

Telephoning

3

Kick-off: Talking to people on the phone

Task

Discuss your experience in class:

In the office …
- … how often do you answer the phone each day?
- … how often do you speak English on the phone?
- … do you find it difficult to answer or make a phone call in English?
- … do you normally speak English to native or non-native speakers of English?

Aims

You learn …
… how to cope with different kinds and phases of phone calls
… how to deal with messages, appointments, arrangements and problems
… how to be a professional phone-communicator
… how to keep control of a conversation with a native speaker
… how to deal with an answering machine and a mobile phone
… how to deal with complaints

Topics

Topic 1: Who, why, when and then?

Task 1

Listen to the dialogue and try to make out the information Mareike Schmitz (caller) gives.

Information given by Mareike Schmitz:
- *greeting*
- …
- …
- …
- …

3 Unit

Task 2

Mareike Schmitz is making several phone calls this morning.
Listen to them and identify where she calls, whom she speaks to, what she wants and what will happen next.

	Call 1	Call 2
Where does she call?		
Whom does she want to speak to?		
What does she want?		
What will happen next?		

Calling

Expression Bank

Giving your name and the name of your company
- Good morning, Sarah Jones speaking./This is Sarah Jones from RTL Creation in Cologne.

Giving the reason for your call
- I am calling about …
- The reason I am calling is …
- I would like to/Could I speak to Celia Hanson, please?
- I am returning Ms Smith's call.
- I would like to speak to somebody in your customer service department, please.

Answering a call

Expression Bank

Telephone switchboards of big companies:
- BBC London, good morning. How can I help you?

Within a big company the department is used in the answer:
- Marketing department, Jane Britain speaking.

In a small company:
- Miller PR. Good morning. This is Jane Britain speaking.

Additions:
- How can I help you?/What can I do for you?
- May I ask who is calling, please?/Could you give me your name, please?
- Thank you for calling back.
  getting back to me.
  returning my call.

Unit 3

Task 3

Listen to the three dialogues again and complete the missing words:

1. ______________________. Jigsaw plc.
   What ______________________?
2. ______________________ Mareike Schmitz ______________________.
3. ______________________ Cologne in Germany.
4. How ______________________?
5. ______________________ to John Edwards in ______________________, please.
6. ______________________, Richard is in a meeting at the moment.
   Can I ______________________?
7. No, thank you. I ______________________.
8. You are ______________________.
9. You will need to talk to Celia Hanson about that. I will ______________________.
10. Okay. ______________________.

Info Point

Try to smile when taking up the receiver: If you record yourself you will "hear" the positive atmosphere you create.

Task 4

Work in pairs and take a turn in the roles.

1. Student A is Heike Kruse from Bode Kommunikation in Cologne, Germany. At a marketing fair in London she has met Jane French (student B) from the agency Marketing Communication in York. Heike rings Jane's agency and asks the receptionist to speak to her. Her line is engaged.
2. Student A is John Smith, operator at the BBC London. Thomas Müller (student B) from Radio Munich in Munich, Germany, calls. Thomas Müller wants to talk to Carol Bone who turns out to be on holiday. John Smith takes his name and message.
3. Student A is Paul Heinze, journalist writing for the Frankfurter Allgemeine Zeitung in Germany. He is interested in the latest press release issued by British Airways as he wants to write an article about the latest developments of international airlines. He calls the company in order to find out the name and extension of the person who is most suitable to talk to about it. He talks to the receptionist Linda Clark (student B).

Closing a call

Expression Bank

- I think that was all.
- Thank you for the information/for your help.
- I am in a meeting at the moment./I have an appointment in a few minutes.
- Can I call you back?
- I will check that and get back to you.
- I look forward to hearing from you soon./Hope to see you soon./We'll be in touch next week.
- Ok, I think that is it.
- Thank you for calling.
- Goodbye.

Checking information

Expression Bank

- Sorry, I didn't catch that. Could you repeat it, please?
- Can I read that back to you?
- So that's 0049 221 4758612.
- Could I just make sure that I've got that right?
- Sorry, I didn't hear that properly.
- Did you say 245 or 249?
- Let me just check that.
- May I repeat that?
- Would you mind repeating that?/Could you just say that again, please?
- Is that B as in butter?
- Could you just spell that for me, please?
- I'll just spell that for you.

Task 5

Unfortunately, the following conversation has got mixed up. Please put the lines in the correct order.

1. I'm afraid he's not in the office this afternoon. Can I give him a message?
2. Yes, please. Can you tell him Jane English rang? I'll try again later.
3. Sponsorpartners Ltd.
4. Goodbye.
5. 05463-7224465. Fine. I'll make sure he gets the message.
6. Good afternoon. Virgin Entertainment Inc.
7. Ms English. OK. Which company are you calling from?
8. Yes, it's 05463-7224465.
9. You're welcome. Goodbye.
10. Good afternoon. Could I speak to James Little, please?
11. Thank you very much.
12. And could you give me your number, please?

Info Point

When somebody thanks you for doing something, it is a typical German mistake to answer "please" for the German „bitte". It is much better to answer "You are welcome", "Not at all" or "That is no problem".

Task 6

In the calls you listened to there were many different names and numbers. As you do not have the time to look things up in a dictionary while you are on the phone, it is important to know about the international conventions beforehand.
Test yourself in order to find out how good you are already:
How do you say the following?

1. January 2, 2012
2. 11.4 %
3. EUR 1 000,000,000
4. s_mueller@wdr-koeln.de
5. Deutsche Post
6. (0049) 2233 109860
7. $11m^2$
8. 5/8
9. $4.6m
10. 9:30 Uhr

3 Unit

Info Point

There are international conventions for saying numbers, dates and the time and for spelling words in order to be understood everywhere in the world. Besides, it is helpful to know about the time zones before making an overseas call. Have a look at the skill file for telephoning (page 148).

Task 7

Christine Heinz works for a marketing agency in Hamburg. She was in a meeting and had several phone calls during that time. The receptionist took the messages but made mistakes in her notes. Listen to the calls and correct the notes.

Telephone Message	Telephone Message	Telephone Message
Call from:	**Call from:**	**Call from:**
Tracy Miller	*Peter Jones*	*Jane French*
Message:	**Message:**	**Message:**
Asks to be called back at Channel 5: 0033 4556 8608931	He will be away from BBC Worldservice January 1 to 2. His replacement will not be available until January 7.	The business lunch of OUP will take place at Gilly's Restaurant in London on Thursday at 1:30 pm.

Info Point

If you have to convey "**bad**" **news** such as the absence or unavailability of a person the caller would like to speak to, it is common to "soften" the news by using respective vocabulary such as "**I'm sorry**" or "**I'm afraid**" to express your regret: "I'm sorry, but Ms Jenkins is on holiday until next Monday and Ms Britain is not available either, I'm afraid" sounds much more polite and friendly than saying "Ms Jenkins and Ms Britain are not available".

The same goes for using **"actually"**: It is used when you want to avoid a "no", when you want to change the subject or when something might be inconvenient or annoying for the person you are talking to and you want to express it in a polite way. "I won't be in the office tomorrow, actually", "Listen, Ms Parker, I would actually like to speak to Mr Miller", "Can I call back later? I'm actually in a meeting at the moment".

Task 8

A caller (employed at a German marketing agency) wants to talk to Jenny Smith at Granada Television in London to discuss the marketing of their latest documentary because his client cooperates with Granada Television in this project and he is responsible for the marketing in Germany. She turns out not to be in the office.
As the caller, work together with your partner who answers the call by representing the operator of Granada Television switchboard. Take turns to play each role.

Operator	**Caller**
Answer the phone as the operator of the Granada Television switchboard.	Greet the person who has answered the call. Introduce yourself and ask for Jenny Smith in the marketing department.
Check who the other person is.	Clarify who you are and why you are calling.
Express your regret that Jenny Smith is not available. Say why (holiday until next Monday) and offer to take a message.	Ask to be called back on her return and leave your telephone number.
Agree, spell the caller's name and check the telephone number.	Close the call and ring off.
Thank the caller and close the call, too.	

Making a connection

Expression Bank

- Who is calling, please?
- Sorry what was your name?
- Can I just ask what it is about?
- Could you please hold?
- One moment, please. I will try to put you through to John Wisker.
  I will connect you to the customer service department.
- I am afraid, there is no answer.
  the line is busy. Would you like to hold?
  she is on the other line.
  she is not available at the moment.
  she is in a meeting/at lunch/not in the office today, at the moment/on holiday/ill.

- It is alright. Thank you. I will call back later.
- OK, I would like to leave a message.

- Can I help you perhaps?
- May I take a message?
- Can I give him a message?
- Would you like to try again later?
- Can I ask her to call you back?
- Does she have your number?
- Could I take your number, please?
- Is it urgent?
- If it is urgent, I can get a message to her at the conference.
- Would you like to speak to someone else?

Task 9

Please decide when and why each of the phrases below is used in a telephone conversation.
Please select at least six phrases and include them in a role-played telephone conversation. Work together with your partner.

a) *Good morning! Harrods Ltd.*

b) *It's my pleasure.*

c) *Jim Smith speaking.*

d) *Good morning, this is Carol Jenkins from Siemens in Munich.*

e) *Sorry, I can't help.*

f) *I'm not getting an answer.*

g) *Just a moment, please.*

h) *Would you like to try again later?*

i) *I'm afraid we just got cut off.*

j) *I think she may have already left.*

k) *It's a very bad line. Would you call again, please? I'll give you her extension.*

l) *Speaking.*

m) *Celia Brown here.*

n) *Can I give her a message?*

o) *Would you like to try again later?*

p) *Could you hold the line, please?*

q) *Could I speak to Jane Kay, please?*

r) *Goodbye and have a nice day.*

s) *Can I repeat that to make sure I got it right?*

t) *Her line is engaged. I cannot connect you right now, I'm afraid. Can we ring you back?*

u) *There is a lot of noise in this line. Could you say that again, please?*

v) *Do you mind sending a fax/an e-mail? I think it might be better.*

w) *I'm afraid you've got the wrong extension.*

x) *Isn't that 3986534? Sorry to have troubled you.*

y) *I'm sorry I didn't get that. Would you mind speaking more slowly, please?*

z) *Could I have the marketing department, please?*

Task 10

Work in pairs and take a turn in the roles.
Imagine you are making a phone call and talk to a business partner about your latest sales figures or the company's performance in general (Compare the unit on meetings, page 99).
Additionally, you also want to confirm the details of the upcoming conference and fix the times of the next meetings.
The phrases-section might help you in finding the right words to express your needs.

1. Please plan and note down for yourself which information you want to communicate (ten pieces).
2. Please also "plan" some problems that might occur in your conversation such as technical interference and problems with figures and spelling.

Leaving a message

Expression Bank

- I would like to leave a message for John Brown.
- Could I leave a message on his voicemail, please?
- Could you ask him to call me back, please?
- I think he has my number but I will give it to you just in case.
- Could you give him my best wishes and say that I will try to call him again next week?
- Could you give Jane Kay a message from me, please?

Using a mobile phone

Expression Bank

- Can you hear me?
- Where are you?
- Is this a good time to talk?
- Have you got a couple of minutes?
- Are you still there?
- What was that beeping noise?
- You're breaking up a little.
- My battery's low – we might get cut off, I'm afraid.
- I think I'm loosing the connection. I'd better go.
- I'm actually on the train. Could you possibly call me on my landline in an hour?

Topic 2: Behaving professionally on the phone – Telephone etiquette

When you answer the phone at work you represent your company to the caller. Important questions are:
How do you
- create a positive image of your employer?
- give the best possible service to your client or business partner?
- maintain a good business relationship with him?

Task 1

Listen to the dialogue and decide whether Andrea Caspari makes a good professional phone-communicator. Give reasons and discuss your answers. Decide how the conversation could be improved in terms of customer care.

Task 2

Make a list of criteria characterising successful behaviour on the phone. Work together with your partner:

A satisfied client or business partner should

- be referred to by name
- …
- …
- …
- …
- …
- …
- …

Telephoning in business situations is not just about talking business. It is also important to create a positive atmosphere in order to prepare the ground for a good business relationship. You can do that by conducting so-called **bonding chats**. Topics for bonding chats could be health (on the surface), the weather, family or current news.

Info Point

There are conventions for making small talk which are helpful to know when you try bonding with your telephone partner. Have a look at the skill file for small talk to avoid any pitfalls. It is also important to know when and how to change from chatting to business (pages 145).

Task 3

Work in pairs:

1. Write down possible beginnings for a conversation.
2. Think about how you can move on from the greeting and initial friendly chat to the main message or reason for a call to avoid talking too much and missing the point of the call. Write down suitable phrases.
3. You receive a call from a colleague or client you know very well. Role-play a possible telephone conversation by using your notes for bonding chats and the following move-over to the business part of the conversation.

Even the most professional phone-communicator might sometimes be confronted with problems such as having to deal with a bad line, asking someone to repeat information or just being very busy and having to say so. In those situations it is especially important not to be too direct but polite. This cannot only be achieved by just sounding friendly, but also by "softening" your language. Additionally there are also certain phrases to be used in such a situation. Altogether, employing active listening strategies helps to communicate effectively on the phone and gives your conversation partner the feeling that you are interested and understanding.

Task 4

Listen to the dialogue and try to find out what makes it so special with regard to language use.

Keeping control when talking to native speakers

Even if you have a good proficiency of speaking and understanding English, it might become hard when you have a native speaker at the other end. The pace can often get very fast and you might run into the problem of losing track of the conversation. But this is no reason to give up: There are a couple of strategies to keep control of a conversation with a native speaker.

Info Point

Interrupting
Even though interrupting may appear to be rude, it is much better to do so than to force your conversation partner to return to what he said five minutes before. By saying **"Sorry?"** or **"Pardon?"** you indicate that you have a problem keeping up.

Slowing down
Native speakers often speak too quickly. When reminded of it they usually slow down for a couple of sentences but pick up speed again soon. **"Could you please speak a bit more slowly?"** is a polite way of reminding your conversation partner of your problem.

Topic 3: How to deal with an answering machine – Leaving and recording messages

Having a technical device answering your call is something many people feel uncomfortable with – especially when they have got to use a foreign language.

Task 1

1. Listen to the message on CD.
2. Write down the information which is given there.
3. Prepare a general message for your employer.
4. Turn it into your own message for the answering machine in your company when someone rings your extension.
5. You would like to talk to John Smith in the company mentioned above in order to enquire about a certain radio programme. Please give an appropriate response and leave your name, number and when he can get hold of you in your office the following day.

From what you have just heard and produced, please write down how you would structure a message you leave on an answering machine and which sentences you would use to express it:

What do you want to express?	How do you say it?
...	...

Making and changing arrangements

Expression Bank

- I would like to fix an appointment/schedule a meeting/set up a meeting for next Monday.
- I was wondering if you might have time next Tuesday.
- Let me just check my diary.
- What about meeting in May?
- Would next Friday suit you?
- Yes, Friday would be fine with me.
- Good, shall we pencil in Friday noon then?
- Actually, I'd prefer the morning, if you don't mind.
- How about Monday instead?
- Would you mind meeting an hour later/earlier?
- Shall I come over to your place or shall we meet over here?
- Fine, so that's 10 am on Monday in your office.
- Could you possibly confirm it in an e-mail?
- Let me also give you my mobile number in case there's a problem and you need to get hold of me.
- I wanted to ask if we could possibly postpone/reschedule/cancel our meeting.
- I'm afraid my meeting has taken longer than I expected.
- I might be running late a few minutes.
- I should be there by 1.30 pm at the latest, but I'll call you again if there are any more delays.

Info Point

When you leave a message on an answering machine, remember to speak slowly and clearly. Repeat the most important details such as your name and number at the end, so people do not have to listen to the message twice in order to get those details.

Task 2

In the meantime, John Brown from BBC Media UK has returned your call. Unfortunately, you have not been in the office and therefore he has left a message. Listen to the message and translate its content into German in order to inform your colleague, who doesn't know English very well, about it.

Topic 4: "Can you hear me?" – Communicating via mobile phone

Task 1

The mobile phone: some people love it, others hate it. What do you think? Are there any dos and don'ts people should follow when using their mobile? Discuss in class.

Task 2

1. Listen to the following conversation and try to write down phrases typical of a conversation on the mobile phone.
2. Role-play the following situation together with your partner by using the phrases from the expression banks in this unit.

Making a telephone call

You are
yourself from the event agency Computas Events in Cologne.

You call
the marketing department of the department store Harrods in London. You want to talk to the event manager Peter Jones since you would like to book their food hall in order to celebrate Michael Schuhmacher's birthday. You get Peter Jones on his mobile.

Problems

Expression Bank

- I am sorry, I did not catch your name.
- And where are you calling from, please?
- I'm sorry. I must have dialled the wrong number.
- I'm sorry, could you just speak a little more slowly, please?
- Could you just speak up a bit/speak a bit louder, please?
- I'm sorry, I didn't catch/get that.
- What was that again/could you just repeat that, please?
- I won't keep you long.
- I am afraid, it is a very bad line. Could you please try again?
- Sorry, we were cut off.
- I'll call you back on the fixed network.
- I'm sorry, I'm on my way to an appointment. Can I call back later?
- The number you called has not been recognised.
  is no longer available.

Topic 5: "I'm terribly sorry about that." – How to deal with complaints

When working together with many different clients every day, you might have to deal with a complaint occasionally. Such a situation is difficult especially on the phone and therefore requires certain instincts in order to make sure that your long-term client is still with you afterwards and that a new client would still recommend you to other potential clients as a competent and professional company.

Task 1

1. Listen to the telephone conversation and discuss how the person called deals with the customer.
2. Make a list of criteria you should take care of when you receive a call from a complaining customer.

Somebody dealing with a complaint should

- let the customer explain the complaint and context
- ...
- ...
- ...

3. In pairs rewrite the telephone conversation between Felix Binse and Celia Snow observing the rules you set up in task 2.

Obviously, Felix Binse has to act fast if he wants to maintain a positive business relationship (see above). After having talked to his colleague, he has found out that there had been a problem with the delivery company in the Netherlands. It had received a wrong order number as Peter Schmitz had made a mistake in the computer system. Therefore, there appears to be a delay in delivery. He intends to write a respective e-mail to Ms Snow after having tried to reach her over the phone without success.

4. Write an e-mail he could send to Ms Snow in order to explain the situation and work on a good business relationship.
5. Practice how to behave in such a situation by role-playing the following telephone conversations together with a partner.

Filing a complaint

Student A
Richard Saunders, marketing manager at Toyota in Cologne calls Sabine Kreihe.
He complains about the decoration he has received for the celebration of the latest Toyota model. It doesn't correspond to what he has negotiated.

Student B
Sabine Kreihe who works for Balloony, decoration supplier, receives a complaint by Richard Saunders. She tries to solve the problem and to still keep him as a happy customer.

6. Pay special attention to language use: How could you "translate" the aspects you identified above into phrases suitable in such a situation?

Dealing with complaints

Expression Bank

- I am awfully/terribly sorry about ...
- I would like to apologise for ...
- Please accept my apologies for ...
- I'm afraid there is a slight problem.
- Unfortunately it seems/appears that there has been a mistake.
- A small/slight problem
- A bit of a problem
- I'll make sure that the problem gets sorted out immediately.
- You should have it by tomorrow at the latest.

Filming permits and applications

If you want to shoot a film outside a studio, i.e. in a public place or privately owned estate, you will have to get a filming permit from the town council or owner. Most cities have application forms for filming permits that you can get from the local government. Here is one example from the City of Westminster (London):

***** Please FAX back this form to +44 (0)20 7641 2640 *****

City of Westminster

Application for

Filming in the City of Westminster

- Please identify the filming officer you have spoken to (if applicable): ____________________
- Please check our website (address at bottom of page) to ensure you have the latest version of this form and our guidance notes for filming on the public highway in Westminster

APPLICANT'S DETAILS

Contact name:		Application date: *(dd/mm/yy)*	
Company:		Fax no:	
Address:		Tel no:	
E-mail:		Mobile no:	
Proof of payment attached? *(if applicable - see charging policy)*		☐ Yes	☐ No

PROPOSED FILMING DETAILS

Production title:		
Filming dates: *(dd/mm/yy)*	/ / to / /	No. of shooting days:
Start/Finish times:	*Interior:*	*Exterior:*
Location of filming operation: *(list all streets & postcodes)*		

Type of operation: *(check as appropriate)*

☐ Feature Film	☐ TV	☐ Outside Broadcast	☐ Radio
☐ Commercial	☐ Music Video	☐ Online/Viral	☐ Photoshoot

☐ Other: *(e.g. Student short; Corporate)* ____________________

Genre: *(e.g. Period; Documentary; Vox pops)* ____________________

Approximate number of ALL personnel "on location/on site":

Please indicate if any of the following will be used on the public highway:

☐ *Handheld camera*	☐ *Camera on tripod*	☐ *Camera on jib/ladderpod*
☐ *Steadicam*	☐ *Camera on dolly track*	☐ *Wet down/rain machine*
☐ *Handheld light(s)*	☐ *Light(s) on stand(s)*	☐ *Light(s) on tower(s)*

FILM LONDON

Filming Application Form

This form is available on our web site at www.westminster.gov.uk/filming *Page 1*

*** Please FAX back this form to +44 (0)20 7641 2640 ***

City of Westminster

Please indicate if any of the following will be used on the public highway:

☐ *Crane* ☐ *Cherrypicker/Access Platform* ☐ *Genie Boom* ☐ *Scissor lift*

*** If yes, please complete the specific platform operations application at the end of this form. Note there is a separate charge and timeframe to process requests for this equipment ***

Please explain <u>in detail</u> each scene to be filmed. A plan should accompany each scene/location, identifying position of all filming equipment:
(NB If you do not provide sufficient detail we will not be able to process your application)

Please indicate if any of the following feature in any exterior scene:

☐ *Use of the public* ☐ *Scene of crime* ☐ *Scene of an offensive nature* ☐ *Violence*

☐ *Firearms* ☐ *Marked Police Car* ☐ *Other Emergency Service vehicle*

☐ *Actors in Police uniform* ☐ *Actors in other Emergency Service uniform*

☐ ***ANY** other equipment, special effects, street dressing requirements or stunts (please specify):*

Please send evidence of your current Public Liability Insurance cover with your application

FILM LONDON

Filming Application Form
This form is available on our web site at www.westminster.gov.uk/filming *Page 2*

The full application can be found on www.westminster.gov.uk/filming.

Task 1

Understanding a filming application

Answer the following questions about the City of Westminster's filming application:

a) *Can you explain the different types of operations listed?*

b) *Can you explain the words 'dolly', 'crane' and 'cherrypicker'?*

c) *What is meant by interior/exterior start and finish times?*

Task 2

Inquiring for a filming permit on the phone

Alpha Film GmbH want to apply for a filming permit in Westminster City (cf. filming application on pages 61–62). Therefore, they call the filming officer of the City of Westminster.
Work in pairs and roleplay the telephone conversation between Alpha Film and the filming officer. Follow the scheme below and invent any details you require:

Filming Officer	**Alpha Film**
Answer the phone as the filming officer of Westminster City (use your own name).	Greet the person who answered the call. Introduce yourself and ask whether he/she is the right person to talk to about a filming permit.
Answer in the affirmative.	Explain what exactly you plan to do, how long it is going to take, etc.
Tell the caller that this should not be a problem but that he has to use the filming application. Tell him where he can find it and that he needs to send it at least six weeks prior to filming.	Say that you have already had a look at it. Ask how detailed the description of each scene should be.
Say that it should include everything that can be found in the script breakdown.	Ask whether it would be enough to enclose the script breakdown.
Answer in the negative. It needs to be written in the application.	Ask for the fees.
State the caller a price of £50 per day.	Thank the officer for the information and close the call.
Thank the caller for calling and offer him to be of future assistance.	Thank again and ring off.

Daily business on the phone

Task 3

Marc Berger, assistant director of the movie *Tropenhitze*, a German-Jamaican co-production, gets a phone call from Ann Taylor, the Jamaican location manager. Complete Marc's part of the conversation with your own words.

Marc: …

Ann: Hi, this is Ann Taylor, location manager for Tropical Heat in Jamaica. Can you help me with some information concerning the shooting schedule?

Marc: …

Ann: Good, I need to know the date of your next shot in Trinidad because I have to plan the rental of the technical equipment.

Marc: …

Ann: Right, that's fine. One more question: how much budget is there for lighting equipment? That's important to know if I want to plan the technical equipment.

Marc: …

Ann: Okay, I'll try his mobile. But just in case I don't catch him, would you be so kind as to tell him I rang and call me back as soon as possible, please?

Marc: …

Ann: Thanks, goodbye then.

Marc: …

Task 4

Listen to the conversation between an A&R representative and a musician. Then answer the following questions:

a) *What does Rob Owen ask for?*

b) *Why can't Stephanie Willows give him an answer yet?*

c) *What do you think will happen next?*

d) *If you work in the music business, is this situation familiar to you? If so, explain it to the other students.*

Task 5

Find the English equivalents of the following German telephone phrases.

Film/TV:

1. Ach, wie gut, dass ich Sie erreiche. Ich muss Sie dringend wegen der Drehgenehmigung im Hyde Park sprechen.
2. Könnten Sie mich bitte mit der Requisiteurin verbinden?
3. Bitte kümmern Sie sich darum, dass der Drehplan morgen vorliegt.
4. Kann ich Sie zurückrufen? Ich muss erst in der Dispo nachschauen.

Musik/Radio:

5. Wir hätten gerne die Rechte, um Robbie Williams' *Angel* auf einem Sampler zu veröffentlichen. An wen kann ich mich deswegen wenden?
6. Wir planen gerade die England-Tournee für Robbie Williams. Könnten Sie mir bitte ein Verzeichnis aller Musikstadien und Konzertsäle in Großbritannien schicken?
7. Wenn sich die CD gut verkauft, können wir bei dem nächsten Album darüber nachdenken, einen Künstlervertrag abzuschließen.
8. Wir sind ein neuer Radiosender in Hamburg. Könnten Sie uns bitte in ihren Verteiler für Robbie Williams-CDs mit aufnehmen?

Dealing with a complaint

Mistakes happen – even with highly-organised business procedures. As companies would like to make sure that dissatisfied customers turn into satisfied ones again, it is necessary to deal with complaints in a polite and helpful way.

The following note was left on your desk:

> *Hi ...,*
>
> *one of our best customers, FastPrint plc in England (+444728583925) has just been complaining by telephone that their enquiry of August 9, 2012 has not been answered. As I am in a hurry, please phone FastPrint, apologise and tell them that our letter was dispatched yesterday, and due to the holiday season there have been delays. Offer them to send the offer again by fax or e-mail.*
>
> *Thanx,*
>
> *...*

Task

Write a short script of what to do and say in a telephone conversation dealing with complaints. You may use the phrases on page 60.

Telephone practice in the advertising business

Sometimes in business-to-business communication a telephone-call is much quicker and more immediate than a letter. However, even if this means of communication seems to be more spontaneous at first sight, there are still rules to be followed in order to make sure that there are no misunderstandings during and after the call.

Task 1

You are in the agency team designing the commemorative brochure and menu card for Jenny's Office Break (compare unit 2, pages 41–42). Instead of writing a letter of complaint because of the faulty delivery, make a phone call to ImPrint Ltd.

a) *Role-play the dialogue between your agency and ImPrint Ltd. Consider the following pieces of information:*
   - There are only three days left until the brochures have to be handed over to Jenny's Office Break.
   - ImPrint needs four days to make the corrections plus one day for delivery.

b) *Also role-play the follow-up call between your agency and Jenny's Office Break telling them that you will not be able to keep the deadline.*

Task 2

For a marketing brochure your agency is currently designing, you need photos from your client in a high resolution (300 dpi). You have already received some pictures but their quality is not good enough for printing. The client has little technical understanding – explain to him exactly what you need and why you need it.
Also offer to send a photographer in order to take new pictures.

Role-play the dialogue between your agency and the client. Make use of your professional experience in order to make up any more details you might need for the conversation!

Task 3

Find the English equivalents of the following German telephone phrases.

1. Ich rufe an wegen Ihres Briefings. Wir hätten da noch ein paar Rückfragen.
2. Könnten Sie uns bitte Bilder und Texte für die Pressemitteilung per e-Mail schicken?
3. In welchem Dateiformat benötigen Sie sie denn?
4. Ich habe Ihnen gerade die Rohfassung per e-Mail geschickt – bitte schauen Sie doch mal bezüglich Satz und Farben darüber.
5. Wenn Sie noch Änderungswünsche haben, können wir gerne Korrekturen vornehmen.

Making arrangements on the phone

Especially when you would like to contact a person for the first time, a telephone call is often the best thing to do. In what follows you will practise how to make acquaintances and arrangements.

Task 1

Practise your small talk skills
Work together with a partner and role-play the situation.

Situation:
You have attended the reception of the international trade fair "World of Events" in Wiesbaden. There you got to talk to several attendants whom you had not met before. As there is the opportunity to do business together, you phone your new acquaintance to arrange an appointment.

You are 1
... yourself from the event agency Sports Events in Cologne.
You talk to
... the event manager Jenny Clark of Harrods Ltd in London who is in Germany for the first time.

You are 1
... Jenny Clark, event manager of Harrods Ltd in London who is in Germany for the first time.
You talk to
... an apprentice of the event agency Sports Events in Cologne.

You are 2
... yourself from Pfefferschote Catering GmbH in Cologne.
You talk to
... Peter Strong, marketing assistant at the PR agency Webber Shandwick Ltd in London.

You are 2
... Peter Strong, marketing assistant at the PR agency Webber Shandwick Ltd in London.
You talk to
... an apprentice from Pfefferschote Catering GmbH in Cologne.

You are 3
... yourself from the decoration shop and service Balloony GmbH in Cologne.
You talk to
... Pierre Cadeau from France who works as an event management clerk at Paris airport Charles de Gaulle.

You are 3
... Pierre Cadeau from France working as an event management clerk at Paris airport Charles de Gaulle.
You talk to
... an apprentice from the decoration shop and service Balloony GmbH in Cologne.

Task 2

General Enquiry

Work together with a partner and role-play the phone call resulting from the e-mail below.

From: Pamela Jones
To: msmith@artists.co.uk
Cc:
Bcc:
Subject: Magician for exam reception
Attachments:

Dear Mr Smith

Your agency has been recommended to me by my colleague Jessica Parker. She has booked performance artists from your office several times in the past and was always highly satisfied with their performances.

This time we would need a magician who is to perform at the exam reception of our students studying events January 6 next year. It is going to take place in the great hall of the institute in Bath Road. You are invited to visit us to check the location.

Could you please give me an overview of what is possible on such an occasion? You can get hold of me in our main office at the institute in Bournemouth at 8608931.

Thank you very much in advance.

Pamela Jones
Marketing-Co-ordinator

The Arts Institute Bournemouth

Task 3

Specific enquiry

You are in the agency team organising the launch of Jenny's Office Break (compare unit 2, pages 41). Unfortunately, there has been a fire at Harrods so that the food hall you have originally enquired about (compare task 2, page 43) will not be available for the event on the planned date.
Call the London local authority to find out whether you could celebrate the event at Covent Garden in one corner of the square which would have to be shut off from the public. Work in pairs and role-play the resulting telephone conversation.

Task 4

Complaining on the phone

Practise your skills to deal with a complaining customer or to complain yourself. Work in pairs.

You are 1
... yourself from the event agency Events Unlimited in Cologne.
You call
... the marketing department of the Queen in London. You want to talk to the event manager James Lost as you have booked the front courtyard of Buckingham Palace in order to celebrate the birthday of Boris Becker.
Problem
You need to change the date of the event. Mr. Lost is not in. You leave a message with Lynn Summer, the assistant of James Lost.

You are 1
... Lynn Summer, the assistant of James Lost, event manager in the marketing department of the Queen in London.
You are called
... by ____ from the event agency Events Unlimited in Cologne. They have booked the front courtyard of Buckingham Palace in order to celebrate the birthday of Boris Becker.
Problem
They want to change the date of the event. Mr. Lost is not in and therefore you have to tell them that the new date they want is not possible.

You are 2
... yourself from Aubergine Catering in Cologne.
You call
... Jane English, sales assistant at Ford Europe in Cologne.
Problem
You want to negotiate the food for the event celebrating the sale of the one millionth Fiesta in Europe. She had mentioned it before but hadn't specified it and now time is running short as the event is to take place in a week.

You are 2
... Jane English, sales assistant at Ford Europe Cologne.
You are called
... by ____ from Aubergine Catering in Cologne.
Problem
He/She wants to negotiate the food for the event celebrating the sale of the one millionth Fiesta in Europe. You had mentioned it before but hadn't specified it and now time is running short as the event is to take place in a week.

Task 5

Find the English equivalents of the following German telephone phrases.

1. Wann werden Sie auf der Buchmesse in Frankfurt sein? Dann können wir uns über die Autorenlesungen unterhalten, die wir in Deutschland organisieren.
2. Guten Tag, hier ist Christina Mint von Webbershandwick in Bonn. Was kann ich für Sie tun?
3. Entschuldigung, ich habe den Namen des Veranstaltungsortes akustisch nicht verstanden. Können Sie ihn bitte buchstabieren?
4. Sie möchten einen Stand für die nächste CeBIT buchen? Einen Moment bitte, ich verbinde Sie mit unserem Auszubildenden Peter Schmidt in der Eventabteilung.
5. Entschuldigung, aber ich bekomme momentan keine Antwort. Möchten Sie über die Bewirtung mit jemand anderem sprechen?
6. Ich würde Sarah gerne eine Nachricht hinterlassen: Wir benötigen für die Party goldene, keine gelben Luftballons.
7. Bist Du noch dran? Ich bin momentan auf dem Weg zur Messe. Soll der Stand 4,5 m oder 5,4 m lang sein?
8. Es gibt ein kleines Problem: Wir können das Veranstaltungskonzept nicht rechtzeitig liefern.
9. Können Sie bitte etwas lauter sprechen? Ich stehe in der Konzerthalle und mein Akku ist schwach. Es tut mir Leid, aber wahrscheinlich ist die Leitung gleich tot.
10. Kann ich Sie zurückrufen? Ich muss erst die Anzahl der Tickets im Computer überprüfen.

Marketing and advertising one's products

4

Kick-off: What is marketing?

Task 1

Have a look at the cartoon – then collect ideas of what marketing is all about in a mind map. Exchange your mind map with a partner and discuss your two versions by making additions on each other's sheet.
To give you an idea of what such a mind map could look like, here is a possible beginning:

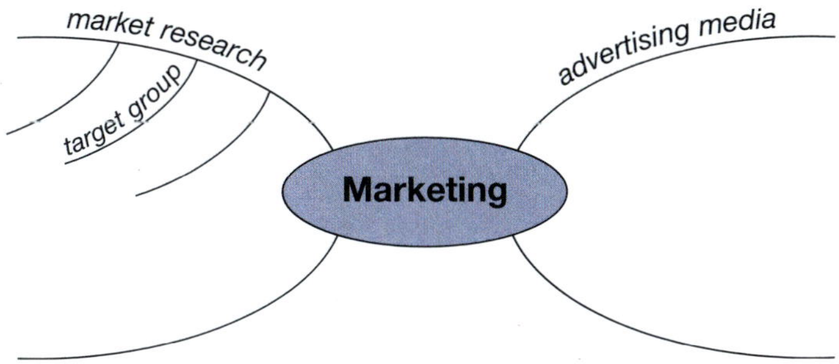

Task 2

Now think of your own company and its products, then answer and discuss the following questions:

- Which target group does your company aim at?
- What position does your company have on the local/national/international media market?
- What is the image of your company and its products?
- Where do you advertise your company and its products?
- What competition do your products face?

Aims

You learn …
… to describe what marketing is about.
… how to distinguish between and use advertising techniques.
… how to use the language of advertising.
… how to analyse TV and print ads.
… how to promote a product.
… how to create a marketing campaign.

Topics

Topic 1: The essence of marketing

Often before a media production has been finished, the question of marketing the product arises. Before you can focus on the question of marketing a media project, some basics of marketing have to be reflected on.

Task 1

Here you find some definitions and ideas on the subject. Read them through, then use them as a basis to formulate your own general definition of marketing.

Marketing is the organisation of the sale of a product, for example, deciding on its price, the shops and areas it should be supplied to, and how it should be advertised.

Marketing is too important to be left to the marketing department of a media company.

In an effective media company organisation, you can't tell who's in the marketing department.

Marketing is getting the right goods and services to the right place at the right time at the right price with the right communication and promotion.

Everyone in a media company has to make decisions based on its impact on the viewers or readers.

The aim of marketing is to know and understand the customers so well that the product or service fits him and sells itself.

Marketing is the creation and delivery of a standard of living.

Marketing is a social and managerial process by which individuals and groups obtain what they need and want through creating and exchanging products and value with others.

Marketing is the performance of business activities that direct the flow of goods and services from producer to consumer.

Task 2

Answer the following questions:

a) *Which statement suggests that everybody in a company is a marketeer?*

b) *Which statement emphasises the role of the four Ps (product, price, place, promotion)?*

c) *Which statement sees marketing to have a more sociological role?*

d) *How would you define the function of marketing in print and audio-visual media?*

Task 3

Marketing vocabulary: "The four P's" and SWOT-analysis

Fill in the gaps in these sentences, using the words from the list.

Words: creative process, design, interview, distribution, end-users, image, labels, mail order, need, opportunities, outlets, place, questionnaire, TV commercials, price, product, satisfy, strengths, threats, weaknesses, competitors', profitably, promotion, customers

1. **Marketing** is the ... of satisfying customer needs ... .
2. The **marketing mix** consists of the "four P's": providing the customer with the right ...., at the right ..., presented in the most attractive way (p...) and available in the easiest way (p...).

3. When doing **market research** you want to find out about your ... using instruments such as a ... or a personal ... .
4. What is a **"product"**? A product is not just a set of components: it is something customers buy to ... a ... they feel they have. The ... and the ... of the product are as important as its features.
5. What is **"price"**? The product must be priced so that it competes effectively with ... products in the same market.
6. What is **"promotion"**? The product is presented to customers through advertising (posters, ..., etc.), packaging (design, ..., etc.), publicity, PR and personal selling.
7. What is **"place"**? Your product must be available to customers through the most cost-effective channels of ... . A consumer product must be offered to ... in suitable retail ..., or available by ... .
8. By **"SWOT analysis"** marketing experts mean that a firm should be aware of its ... and ... and the ... and ... it faces in the market.

Topic 2: Researching the market

The most direct way of finding out how your products or services are evaluated by potential buyers is interview them. Here, you can ask questions in such a way that you get valuable information for testing your marketing-strategies.

Task 1

Listen to the interview and answer the following questions:
- What is the interview about?
- Which is the first question the interviewer asks? What do you think is its function?
- At which point in the interview does the interviewer ask personal questions? Discuss whether this makes sense or whether you would rather ask them at another point.
- Describe the general structure of the interview – can you form groups of questions?
- Finally, describe the type of questions asked, e.g. open or closed questions, ranking or yes-no-questions.

Task 2 A market survey

Step 1: Work with a partner.
In your team, think of a new product or service that your company might want to offer/produce in the future. Then set up a short questionnaire that helps you find out about your classmates' preferences and habits regarding this product/service.

Step 2: Now mill around and lead an interview with at least four students.

Variation: Copy the questionnaire and hand it to all the students in your class so that they can fill it out themselves.

Step 3: Now analyse the data you got, visualise them in a chart or table and present them to the rest of the class. (Refer to unit 5 on meetings and presentations, especially pages 115–118.)

Topic 3: Advertising one's products

A) Advertising Techniques

Companies appeal to consumers in many different ways to persuade them to buy their products. Therefore, they use a variety of advertising techniques, a choice of which is given below. They usually appeal to people's lifestyle, social life or personal fears. Have a look for yourself.

Task 1

Match the advertising techniques with the correct description given in the table and find at least one example for each technique!

avant-garde　before and after
facts and figures (also called science)
hidden fears/guilt　music association
patriotism　snob appeal
transfer/association of ideas
testimonial (endorsement)　wit and humour

Advertising technique	Description	Find an example.
	Customers are attracted to products that divert the audience by giving them a reason to laugh or to be entertained by clever use of visuals or language.	
	The suggestion that using this product puts the user ahead of the times.	

	Some products are shown as having an immediate effect on their users. The situation before using the product is contrasted with the situation after its use.	
	The suggestion that this product will protect the user from some danger. Some ads also evoke the feeling that you might not be doing the best for your loved ones.	
	Some ads use music to create certain moods and thereby evoke emotions and feelings which the user is supposed to associate with the product.	
	Statistics and objective factual information are used to prove the superiority of the product.	
	Words and ideas with positive connotations are used to suggest that the positive qualities should be associated with the product and the user.	
	The suggestion that purchasing this product shows your love of your country.	
	The suggestion that the use of the product makes the customer part of an elite group with a luxurious and glamorous lifestyle.	
	A famous personality is used to endorse the product.	

B) The language of advertising

Did you ever notice that all successful advertising campaigns rely on short and catchy phrases? Here are a couple of well-known examples:

Task 2

a) *Read the advertising slogans above and guess what type of product is being advertised.*

b) *What do the slogans promise the customer?*

c) *Point out the most striking features regarding their language. Which words are chosen? Which grammatical form do adjectives and verbs have? Are there any puns? What is the sentence structure like?*

d) *Make a list of all the language features that you think are typical in advertising.*

The language of advertising:

- short sentences
- use of keywords
- …
- …
- …

e) *Think of slogans for the following products using similar rhetorical devices: a pair of shoes, a music CD, a women's magazine, a new Harry Potter novel, a new James Bond movie, a packaging of biscuits.*

C) The AIDA formula

One of the first things you learn when working in the advertising industry is the famous AIDA formula. This formula is the advertisers' recipe for successful advertising. If an advertisement follows the AIDA formula, it will have the ideal effect on the consumer.

A – stands for attention, i.e. the advertisement should be designed so that it grabs the reader's attention.

I – stands for interest, i.e. the reader should not only become aware of the ad, but also become interested in the advertised product.

D – stands for desire, i.e. once the reader has become interested in the advertised product, the advertisement should make him desire to buy the product.

A – stands for action, i.e. if the advertisement has produced its wanted effect, it results in the purchase of the product.

Task 3

Try to find four ads in an English (if possible) or German magazine. Have another look at the slogans in B) and analyse in what way they help to reach the aim of the AIDA formula. Also have a look at the ads you found and say how they make use of the AIDA formula.

D) Analysis of advertisements

Task 4

Have a look at the four advertisements you found and analyse them by doing the following:

1. Identify at least two **advertising techniques** that are used in each advertisement and explain how each of them is used.
2. Identify the **target audience** for each advertisement and explain why you think the advertisement is meant for that group of potential customers.
3. Analyse the **language** used in the ads regarding the choice of words, grammar and sentence structure.
4. Analyse the **design/layout** of the ads and identify the **effect** it has on the readers.
5. Choose the advertisement that you find most convincing and write a seven to eleven sentence paragraph identifying why you would buy the product.

Your teacher will give you a grid which helps you structure your analyses.

Topic 4: The ethics of advertising

There are countless publications on the way in which marketing-campaigns are planned and designed. Doubtlessly one of the funniest – and nevertheless most critical – can be found in Bill Bryson´s *Notes from a Big Country.* In the following excerpt, the author rallies against how Americans are exposed to an incredible amount of (often misleading) advertising.

Commercials, commercials, commercials

There is an advert running on television at the moment that says something like 'The new Dodge Backfire. Rated number one against the Chrysler Inert for handling. Rated number one against the Plymouth Repellent for mileage. Rated number one against the Ford Eczema for repair costs.'

As you will notice, because luckily for you your brain has not been dented and dimmed by years of over-exposure to rapid-fire American advertising, in each category the Dodge is rated against only one other competitor, which makes comparisons a trifle hollow, if not actually suspect. I mean to say, if the Dodge were rated top against ten or twelve or fifteen competitors in any of these categories, then presumably the ad would have said so. Because it doesn't say so, one must naturally conclude that the Dodge performed worse than all its competitors except the one cited. Ergo, it is effectively inviting you to think twice before buying a Dodge.

(...)

Being carefully selective with the truth is venerable tradition in American advertising. I retain a special fondness for a series of ads run by an insurance company in which 'real people in real situations' discussed their personal finances. When a journalist asked the company who these 'real people' were, a spokesman replied that actually they were actors and 'in that sense they are not real people'. That tells you about as much as you need to know about the American approach to advertising.

To be fair, not all American commercials are vacuous or misleading. Quite a lot of them – well two of them – are droll and original. I am particularly taken at the moment with a commercial for pizza by the foot in which a deliveryman with an overlong pizza destroys everything he comes in contact with. (My least favourite, for the record, is one in which a gorgeous-and-don't-I-know-it young woman turns to the camera and says, 'Don't hate me because I'm beautiful.' To which I always reply, 'Oh, I don't. I hate you because you make me gip.')

No, the problem with American commercials is that they are simply so constant. Most channels have a commercial break about every five or six minutes. CNN, as far as I can tell, has nothing but commercial breaks.

It occurred to me that this is rather a sweeping statement, so I have just taken a half-hour, at no extra cost to you, to monitor a typical CNN programme, and here are my findings. In a single 30-minute period, CNN interrupted its programme five times to show twenty commercials.

Altogether it showed 10 minutes of commercials in a 30-minute slot. Apart from a 7-minute span at the start of the programme, the longest period without commercials was 4 minutes and 59 seconds. The shortest interval between commercials was 2 minutes. For the benefit of people who suffered a serious brain injury during the programme, three of the commercials were repeated. This, I hasten to add, is completely typical. Last night, one of the networks showed the movie *The Fugitive*, and I did a similar exercise. In order to watch about 100 minutes of movie, it was necessary to sit through almost 50 minutes of commercials, spread over about twenty interruptions. (One every 7 minutes, on average.)

According to Neil Postman in his book *Amusing Ourselves to Death*, the average American is exposed to 1,000 television commercials a week. By the time he is eighteen, the typical American child has sat goggle-eyed through no fewer than 350,000 television adverts.

Increasingly nowadays even when you are not watching commercials you are watching commercials, so to speak. For example, the ABC network recently aired a special on the making of the Disney movie *The Hunchback of Notre Dame*. According to the *New York Times*, several ABC stations also devoted a portion of their evening news broadcasts to 'a gala celebration that Disney threw for the movie in New Orleans'. It just happens that ABC owns the Disney Company.

Meanwhile, the History Channel unveiled plans to run a series called *The Spirit of Enterprise* celebrating the history and achievements of corporations like Boeing, DuPont and General Motors. The programmes were to be made by – yup – the corporations themselves. The History Channel later cancelled the series when it was brought to its attention that the whole undertaking was just too, too tacky.

(...)

In short, commercials are inescapable here – and not just at home. I am appalled to report that many thousands of schools across America now rely, at least in part, on educational materials provided by corporations, so that pupils are learning about nutrition from McDonald's and conservation and the environment from Exxon, among others. Since 1989, a company called Channel One has been beaming educational programmes to schools via a closed-circuit system. The programmes are free but they are interspersed with commercials aimed specifically at young audiences. Now I would call that obviously, palpably unacceptable and exploitative, but this is evidently a minority view. Channel One has been a big hit; its sets are in 350,000 class-rooms.

Even Sesame Street programmes – this is truly heartbreaking – have become, in the words of the *Boston Globe*, 'uninterrupted 30-minute commercials'. As the Globe points out, Sesame Street products generate over $800 million in retail sales every year, and its executives enjoy salaries of up to $200.000 a year. Yet because the programme is aired on public television here, it receives an annual government subsidy of $7 million.

I was about to say think what would happen if that $7 million were spent instead on inner-city schools, but then it occurred to me that what would happen is that they would go out and buy more TVs to hook more classrooms into Channel One.

Inevitably, this has made my brain throb, so I'm off to take a Tylenol. I understand that in a survey it was preferred over other brands by two to one. Or maybe I'm thinking of Pepsi.

From: Bill Bryson, Notes from a Big Country, Random House Inc., 1999

Words, words, words

air (to) – ausstrahlen
dent (to) – einbeulen
dimmed – verdummt
it makes me **gip** – mir wird übel
goggle-eyed – mit Kulleraugen
mileage – (Sprit)verbrauch
nutrition – Ernährung
over-exposure – übermäßiges Ausgesetztsein
palpably – offenkundig, eindeutig
rapid-fire – schnell aufeinander folgend
for the **record** – der Ordnung halber
subsidy – Unterstützung, Subvention
survey – Umfrage
sweeping – weitreichend
tacky – billig, schäbig
throb – klopfen, pochen
a **trifle** – ein wenig
Tylenol – Eigenname für ein Schmerzmittel
unveil – enthüllen
vacuous – geistlos, ausdruckslos
venerable – altehrwürdig

Task

Answer the following questions.

1. What is a commercial break? Do we have them in Germany?
2. How many minutes per hour of advertising does German TV broadcast?
3. Is there a legal regulation concerning advertising on TV in Germany? Is there one in Great Britain or the US?
4. What does Bill Bryson criticise about advertising? Which of the arguments do you think is the most convincing one?
5. Can you think of any arguments in favour of advertising? Make a list.

Topic 5: Public relations – How to get publicity for your products

Companies use press releases to promote a product or service or to present a positive public image without the costs of advertising. Press releases are usually sent to a wide range of media groups including newspapers, TV- and radio-stations, and the internet. Nowadays, this is often done in electronic format and therefore called EPK – Electronic Press Kit.

Task 1

What should you observe when writing a press release? List at least three items.

- …
- …
- …

Press Release Template

FOR IMMEDIATE RELEASE:

Contact:
Contact Person
Company Name
Telephone + Fax Number
E-mail address
Website address

Headline

City, State, Date – Opening Paragraph (should contain: who, what, when, where, why):

Remainder of body text - should include any relevant information about your products or services. Include benefits, why your product or service is unique. Also include quotes from staff members, industry experts or satisfied customers.

If there is more than one page use: -more-

Abbreviated headline (page 2)

Remainder of text.

For additional information or a sample copy, contact: (repeat contact information)

or – ENDS –
(indicates press release is finished)

How to structure a press release

One of the most important lessons that beginners need to learn is that writing media releases is all about developing a persuasive communication within the framework of a traditional news story format. Editors will not consider press releases that make outlandish promises – "the best ever", "everyone wins", "changing humankind forever." Instead, press release writers should think like a reporter. Press releases should follow journalistic style in order to be given consideration. How do you accomplish this task? Here are some guidelines:

1. **The Headline:** In about ten words – or less – you need to grab the attention of the editor. The headline should summarise the information in the press release, but in a way that is exciting and dynamic; think of it as a billboard along a highway – you have just a few words to make your release stand out among the many others editors receive on a day.
2. **Opening Paragraph:** Sometimes called a summary lead, your first paragraph is critical. This paragraph must explain "the five Ws and one H" of the story – the Who, What, When, Where, Why, and How. This paragraph must summarise the press release, with the following paragraphs providing the details. The opening paragraph must also contain the hook: the one thing that gets your audience interested in reading more – but remember that the hook has to be relevant to your audience as well as to the news media. A hook is not a hard sell or a hidden promotion – it's just a factual statement.
3. **The Body:** Using a strategy called the *inverted pyramid*, the body of the press release should be written with the most important information and quotes first. This inverted pyramid technique is used so that if editors need to cut the story to fit space constraints, they can cut from the end without losing critical information.
4. **The Closing Paragraph:** Repeat the critical contact information, including the name of the person, his or her phone number and/or email address.

Sample press release

PRESS RELEASE

[Headline] **Steve Jobs Resigns as CEO of Apple – Tim Cook Named CEO and Jobs Elected Chairman of the Board**

[Opening paragraph] CUPERTINO, California – August 24, 2011 – Apple's Board of Directors today announced that Steve Jobs has resigned as Chief Executive Officer, and the Board has named Tim Cook, previously Apple's Chief Operating Officer, as the company's new CEO. Jobs has been elected Chairman of the Board and Cook will join the Board, effective immediately.

[Body] "Steve's extraordinary vision and leadership saved Apple and guided it to its position as the world's most innovative and valuable technology company," said Art Levinson, Chairman of Genentech, on behalf of Apple's Board. "Steve has made countless contributions to Apple's success, and he has attracted and inspired Apple's immensely creative employees and world class executive team. In his new role as Chairman of the Board, Steve will continue to serve Apple with his unique insights, creativity and inspiration."

"The Board has complete confidence that Tim is the right person to be our next CEO," added Levinson. "Tim's 13 years of service to Apple have been marked by outstanding performance, and he has demonstrated remarkable talent and sound judgment in everything he does."

Jobs submitted his resignation to the Board today and strongly recommended that the Board implement its succession plan and name Tim Cook as CEO.

As COO, Cook was previously responsible for all of the company's worldwide sales and operations, including end-to-end management of Apple's supply chain, sales activities, and service and support in all markets and countries. He also headed Apple's Macintosh division and played a key role in the continued development of strategic reseller and supplier relationships, ensuring flexibility in response to an increasingly demanding marketplace.

[Closing paragraph] Apple designs Macs, the best personal computers in the world, along with OS X, iLife, iWork and professional software. Apple leads the digital music revolution with its iPods and iTunes online store. Apple has reinvented the mobile phone with its revolutionary iPhone and App Store, and has recently introduced iPad 2 which is defining the future of mobile media and computing devices.

Press Contacts:

Katie Cotton
Apple
katiec@apple.com
(408) 974-72xx

Steve Dowling
Apple
dowling@apple.com
(408) 974-18xx

Source: Apple Press Info, Steve Jobs Resigns as CEO of Apple, 24.08.2011, http://www.apple.com/pr/library/2011/08/24Steve-Jobs-Resigns-as-CEO-of-Apple.html, [7.10.2011]

Task 2

Write a press release about one of your company's latest events/products/services according to the sample and rules mentioned above. This could be:
- the launch of a new CD, film, book, magazine, etc.
- the cooperation with another company
- the announcement of an up-coming event

Project: Creating a marketing campaign

Task 3

Divide the class into groups of four. Following the rules you have learnt about advertising in this chapter, create a marketing campaign for a product of your choice.

If you work in …
… the *film* business, choose a movie that you would like to promote
… the *music* business, choose a CD or an artist that you would like to promote
… the *print* business, choose a magazine, newspaper or book that you would like to promote
… the *event* or *advertising* business, choose a company/a company's product that you would like to promote, or promote your own event/advertising agency

Your marketing concept should be structured in the following way. You can use posters, transparencies or other media in order to visualise your results.

	Content	Example (keywords only)
1. Introduction	Describe the product/company you are going to promote.	Product: Twinings Speciality Teas
2. Target and target group	Describe the target of the campaign and specify the target group.	Target: introduction of new flavour "after dinner mint" to the market Target group: conservative middle-aged and older people, male and female, quality-oriented consumers
3. Claim	Which message should be conveyed through the campaign? Think up a catchy slogan.	Claim: quality, tradition Slogan: "delicious tasting teas – now even easier to discover"
4. Strategy	Which means of communication should be applied? Describe the deployment of different advertising media and public relations. Provide a rough layout of a print, radio or TV advert and write a press release.	TV: spot showing an elderly couple taking their after-dinner tea Print: … Event: … PR: … …
5. Schedule	Set up a timetable containing information when, where and how the elements of your marketing campaign will be put into practice.	One month prior to launch: print campaign One week prior to launch: TV campaign On launch: TV campaign and promotion in tea-rooms …

Case study – Film marketing

The marketing of a film starts six to eight months before the release date[1]. The film's distributor is responsible for its marketing – for bringing the film to the public's attention. Marketing is an expensive business – buying advertising space, producing publicity materials and running promotions all costs money. There have been cases where more money was spent on the marketing of a film than on its production. Many films are released each week and film marketing has become increasingly aggressive as more and more films compete for the same audience. (…) As an audience, how do we become aware of a new film? First of all, we might read an article in a magazine or see the publicity posters. Then we might see a trailer at the cinema, hear an advert on the radio or see adverts in magazines and newspapers. And in the weeks before the film opens, the stars appear on various television programmes promoting the film and the trailer might be shown on television.
This is the marketing campaign from the point of view of the audience. In the weeks before the film opens we are bombarded with 'hype' about the film, the stars, special effects, the soundtrack and genre, all of which influences our decision to buy a ticket.

Text adapted from Film Education, Teacher's Notes, Part One: A Case study-Film Marketing and "Judge Dredd", http://www.filmeducation.org/pdf/film/JDredd.pdf, [20.11.2011]

Example: Lord of the Rings – The Fellowship of the Rings

The marketing campaign for "The Fellowship of the Rings" began with the announcement of New Line Cinema in August 1998 that it will produce a Lord of the Rings trilogy to be made in New Zealand. When in April 2000 an internet preview was launched, this reached a world record of 1.67 million 'hits' in the first 24 hours. In January 2001 the official website was launched and the first trailer released. Four months later, in May 2001, 26 minutes of footage were screened at the Cannes Film Festival to great acclaim of the public. Already in October 2001, two months prior to the world premiere in London, a LOTR fan club was launched.

Example taken from www.mediaed.org.uk/posted_documents/MarketingLOTR.htm, [August 2005]

Task 1

Conduct a survey with the members of your class to find out how and why people decide to see one film rather than another. Is it because of the poster? The trailer? The adverts? The star? The genre? The special effects? The director? It may be a combination of reasons. Interview at least five people, then write up your findings in a report.

[1] Underlined words see vocabulary list on page 92

Film marketing – The process

The distributors' awareness of the film has two stages. Firstly, they are kept informed about forthcoming films going into production. As the film goes into post production and editing, the distributors receive publicity material from the studio; production notes, including background information about the making of the film, credits and biographies of the cast, director and crew; black and white stills and colour slides taken on set by photographers or lifted from the footage of the film. The second stage happens 6–8 months before the release date and involves the marketing team viewing the film followed by a brainstorming session, in which points such as audience research, release date, box office income and advertising budget are discussed.

Raising awareness of the film

The budget of a film marketing campaign is divided into 'above-the-line' and 'below-the-line' costs. The advertising budget is an 'above-the-line' cost, where the distributor pays a certain amount of money to buy advertising space (on television and radio, and in magazines and newspapers). They pay for a slot and know what they are getting for their money. They know the size of the advert, when and where it will be placed and roughly how many people are expected to see it. Publicity and promotion are 'below-the-line' costs – where money is spent on bringing stars from America, for example. The distributor hopes to get good coverage in the media, but this is not guaranteed.

Publicity – Poster and artwork

The poster campaign is the primary medium for selling a film, and will generally start in the early stages of a film's production and continue during the weeks building up to the release.
The poster is the basis of the whole publicity campaign and out of this 'Key Art' or central image come the standees (displayed in cinema foyers), ranges of posters and television adverts.
Artwork for a film poster can either be an original painting based on a key idea in the film or it can be produced from the photographs which are taken during the shoot. The aim in both cases is to find a 'narrative image' that sums up the film. For example, let us say that we have to publicise a comedy-drama about two friends racing across America in vintage cars they have restored themselves. Our stars are Eddie Murphy and Sylvester Stallone, two very popular actors. We will want to show various elements in our poster which include the stars, their vehicles and the fact that the film is a comedy.

The copy

As well as a visual image, posters carry a certain amount of copy (writing), depending upon the stage in the campaign at which they appear. 'Tag lines' are used to underline key elements of the film. Awards won or names of the director or cast can also be used. Quotes from critics and tag lines help reinforce the image and make the poster more effective.

The press kit

Press kits are sent to journalists all over the country to give them information about forthcoming films. They are one of the basic tools of any publicity department. Kits include a set of authorised stills, cast and crew credits, production notes, biographies and filmographies of the cast, director and producer.
In addition to materials sent to print journalists, journalists working in television or radio also receive electronic press kits (EPKs) containing selected video clips and interviews for television, or audio clips for radio.

Star interviews

To promote the film in the weeks leading up to its release, the stars are brought into the country at the distributors' expense. This means paying for flights, travel (usually a chauffeur driven car), hotels, entourage, meals, a daily spending allowance and entertainment. A busy schedule of press interviews and events are planned by the distributors to fully exploit the value of the stars' visit.
When stars are unable to travel, perhaps because of other filming commitments, a press junket will be arranged. These take place in America or the United Kingdom and involve a number of key journalists taking part in a round-the-table interview with the star(s).

Task 2

Design a publicity poster for the film you have chosen in class. Your poster must include:

- The title of the film
- The names of the film's main stars
- Information about the film's director, writer, producers, distributors and music in small print.
- The film's certification
- A 'tag line' that tells us something about the film – something that makes us want to know more. The 'tag line' for the United States campaign for the film 'StarGate' for example was "It will take you a million light years from home – but will it bring you back?" See if you can come up with something as exciting for your film.

Trailer

The trailer starts being played in the cinema around six weeks before the release of a film and runs until the film opens. The trailer aims to raise audience awareness of a film by logging the film title in their minds, give an overall impression of the film to its potential audience and make sure that the audience is aware of the stars. It should also create the desire to see the film when it finally opens. Trailers tend to use a combination of footage from the film, graphics and voice-over to generate curiosity and are usually about sixty seconds long.
Can you recall any trailers that had an impact on you? What was it that made the film stand out in your mind and did you eventually see the film when it was released?

Internet

The internet can be used in various ways in order to get publicity for a film. Firstly, most films have their own website, secondly you can find a variety of reviews on cinema or other film sites. Thirdly, some films have such a great number of fans that these create fan sites.

Example Lord of the Rings

The US movie industry has a long-established practice of shutting down fan sites, or threatening legal action if images are being used. New Line Cinema, in the case of LOTR, instead actively worked with the existing online community, targeting the 400 + LOTR fan sites through 'viral messaging'. The thought was, let's leave the site alone and just become another silo of information on the web. By partnering with fan sites and feeding them 'insider tips', New Line Cinema extended the film's marketing reach to a worldwide audience of tens of millions.

Advertising – Press advertising

The main medium for press advertising is newspapers. The print media advertising campaign usually starts two weeks prior to the opening of the film and for daily and weekly publications advertisements can be booked just a few days in advance.

Task 3

Go to a large international newsagent's to carry out this piece of research. Look at all the papers and magazines which are on display and decide which magazines/ newspapers would be the best place to advertise your film. While you are there, note

down which periodicals carry advertisements, reviews or interviews connected with films. Are there any periodicals or magazines carrying adverts for films that you didn't expect? Why?
Design an advertisement to appear on the outside back cover of a magazine for the film you have chosen in class. Make sure that the main parts of the advertisement (especially the title) can be read from about two metres away. Bear in mind that these act as 'mini posters' that people carry around with them, and think about what a poster needs to convey.

Television advertising

Usually only high budget films can afford a television campaign. The trailer will usually be shown on television 5–10 days before the film is due to open and be repeated during the first week of release. The scheduling of the advert will depend on who the film's target audience is. For example, a horror film can benefit from being shown late at night during related programmes, which are far cheaper than the peak-time spots which reach a wider audience.

Radio advertising

Radio advertising is considerably cheaper than television and is usually used for mainstream films. However, targeted radio stations – a jazz station or a classical station, for example – might be appropriate for the advertising of specialist films. Adverts themselves consist of music from the film and narrative voice-over detailing the venue and release date.

Promotion – Merchandising campaigns

The merchandising deals that can be made from a potential 'blockbuster' are very lucrative and in some cases can even necessitate the setting up of a department which deals solely with merchandising produced for the company's films – toys, clothes and gimmicks such as pencil cases and lunch boxes are now commonplace. In some ways the wearing of the clothes, using the backpack or playing with the toys from the film is a form of advertising, as you are reminding people of and recommending the product.

Example Lord of the Rings

LOTR merchandising began appearing in mid 2000 through deals such as that struck with Toy Biz. Other promotional deals and 'tie-ins' included Burger King and book publishers. New Line Cinema has imposed a strict marketing plan, ensuring that licensed merchandising stays in demand – every font, every drawing, every logo, every image on every product has to adhere to strict style guides consistent with the film.

Task 4

In pairs, script and record a radio advertisement for the film you have chosen in class. If you use two tape recorders or a recorder with over-dubbing facilities you'll be able to use the soundtrack or sound effects from the film and also record the voice-over, which will sound professional. Practise before your final recording. Experiment with the equipment to make sure the volume level is right and for best results, count to ten (silently) after you have pressed the record button before you start speaking. Make sure that you speak at the right speed and experiment with the expression in your voice.

Promotions

Promotions give added awareness to a film and help to reinforce its title. They tend to take the form of joint involvement with another party who will gain from their involvement, for example, a tie-in with Pizza Hut or McDonald's.
Have a look at the shops in your local high street or shopping centre. How many film-linked products can you find? What sort of merchandise is it and what age group is it targeted to? Indeed, can you tell the target age of a film by the merchandise on sale?

Words, words, words

box office income – eingespielter Betrag der Kinos
colour slides – Diapositive
copy – hier: Werbetext
coverage (media) – Berichterstattung (in den Medien)
credits – hier: Abspann (eines Films)
daily spending allowance – Spesen
distributor – hier: Filmverleiher
editing – Schnitt
entourage – Gefolge
footage – Footage, Bildarchivmaterial
junket – sog. Dienstreise auf Kosten anderer
press kit – Pressematerial
release date – Veröffentlichungs-/Erscheinungsdatum
slot – hier: Werbeplatz
stills – hier: Standphotos
tie-in – Verbindung
venue – Veranstaltungsort
vintage cars – Oldtimer
viral – Virus

Marketing a novel

In the following excerpt, American author Jeffrey Marks offers his views on how a novel, in his opinion, should be marketed.

Marketing the genre novel

By Jeffrey Marks

When I started writing, I wasn't sure how to get the message out regarding my book. If enthusiasm was any indication, my first book would have been a best seller. I work in marketing in my day job; certainly, I should have known what to do in order to sell mystery novels. I did know that the world had changed. The dream life of running off to Paris and writing like Hemingway had been replaced with the more proletarian life of sitting in a mall bookstore and directing patrons to the bathroom.

I decided to learn from expert advice and purchased a few of the how-to guides on book marketing and promotion. Most of the books on the market at that time were geared towards non-fiction. These books were helpful when talking about promoting my biographies, but they didn't help much in getting attention for my mysteries.

My next step was to escort a few authors around town and talk to them. Most writers are generous people who are happy to answer questions, and they were grateful for the free car service and a chance to rest their weary signing hand. I met bookstore managers and community relations managers for several stores. These experiences taught me about how to behave during booksignings and media events. I still follow their advice, which really amounts to good manners. Since Cincinnati isn't a literary Mecca, I also wrote author profiles for many years. The experience allowed me to ask writers about their experiences in marketing their works, what worked and what didn't. They were eager to share stories of what had really helped them to get noticed in a very competitive arena.

I began to learn about professional organizations and conferences. I attended a few conferences and made some incredible contacts there. Authors shouldn't wait until their first book hits the shelf to start making these contacts; it's never too early to begin making introductions. For all the websites and real-time activities that can be done to market your work, book promotion still relies heavily on personal contacts and word-of-mouth sales.

I didn't know all of this. Some of it I stumbled into fortuitously. I had to learn other things the hard way. It took a few years and many wrong turns to find the ways that work best when talking about book promotion for fiction. I've done

the dreaded mall signings and even lived to tell about it. They're not that bad if you go into them with a positive attitude and a smile.
Marketing genre fiction is a unique endeavor, but it doesn't have to be something learned by trial and error. After several years of hard knocks, I was asked to write a book on how to promote genre fiction. That book was published in 2002 as Intent to Sell, and is coming out with an updated second edition in April.
That led to me taking over MurderMustAdvertise, a Yahoogroup established to share ideas about book marketing. Many of those ideas have made their way into the new version of the book and into my repertoire of tools for selling books. Helping others to learn about marketing has made me a better promoter as well.
One of the things I've found is that what works for one author might fail miserably for another. I don't mind interacting with readers. After being cooped up for months writing a novel, I'm happy to be out and talking to readers. It's a matter of preference and the author's comfort with selling. Some writers prefer the solitary life and hate the idea of doing any selling.
I hope that I can help other authors find a way to make their voice heard above the din of a thousand other authors. Who knows? It might just be a book I want to read.

Jeffrey Marks, the author of five novels, is the newest instructor at WritersWeekly.com University. His class, Intent To Sell – Marketing Genre Fiction Works In Today's Marketplace, aims to help first-time novelists create the materials they need to go out and set up booksignings, go to genre fiction conventions and even line up television and radio interviews.

Source: Jeffrey Marks, WritersWeekly, Marketing The Genre Novel, 23.02.2005, www.writersweekly.com/this_weeks_article/002440_02232005.html, [24.09.2011] (adapted)

Task

Using the information given by Jeffrey Marks, develop a checklist of ideas how to market a novel.

How to win a contract

When a company or corporation wants to find an advertising agency to create an advertising campaign for one of their products, it has become quite common to call for tenders, i.e. several advertising agencies are invited to come up with an idea and present this idea in a so-called pitch meeting. The agencies compete against each other and the agency with the best idea wins the contract.

Task

Project
A pitch meeting

Now divide the class into groups of four – each group represents an advertising agency and will have to present their ideas in a pitch meeting.

Your preparation time is one hour and the presentation should not last longer than 10 minutes. You can use all available means in order to present your results.

Situation:
United Biscuits, Britain's leading manufacturer of biscuits and chocolates, want to introduce their brand McVitie's to the German market. They have contacted your advertising agency and asked to create ideas for a marketing campaign in Germany. In the pitch meeting your task will be to present your 'agency's' ideas while competing against the other 'agencies' in your class. Prepare a presentation of your ideas detailing which means of promotion you propose. Of course, you don't have to come up with a complete campaign, but you have to convince your client that your agency has the best ideas and is the ideal partner for United Biscuits.

Tip: Use the skill file presentations on page 143 and unit 5 in order to prepare and structure your presentation!

Here is some information about McVitie's from the United Biscuits website. For more information check www.unitedbiscuits.co.uk.

McVitie's – The Original

McVitie's first foray into the blending of biscuit and chocolate resulted in the Homewheat Chocolate Digestive brand (now simply known as McVitie's Chocolate Digestives) in 1925. Over 71 million packets of McVitie's Chocolate Digestives are eaten in the UK each year – that's an astounding 52 biscuits per second.

The HobNobs brand was launched in 1985 and a milk chocolate variant followed in 1987. The chocolate HobNobs range was extended most recently to include HobNobs Creams, and in 2008 the re-introduction of Dark Chocolate HobNobs.

1999 saw the introduction of the innovative tubes packaging for Chocolate Digestives, and the new packaging format was extended to Chocolate HobNobs the following year. 1999 was also the year when the Digestives family was further extended with the launch of Milk Chocolate Caramel Digestives. (...)

Over the last five years, McVitie's biscuits have benefited from a salt reduction programme. For example, McVitie's Digestives have reduced sodium by 26 % (51 % salt reduction) and Hobnobs by 41 % sodium (60 % salt).

In February 2008, McVitie's launched their first ever organic biscuits. Called Yumbles, the yummy crumbly range of biscuits are made from the highest quality organic ingredients and are available in four delicious flavours (...).

The McVitie's brand portfolio also includes McVitie's Minis, Classic Rich Tea, Fruit Shortcake, Ginger Nuts, Boasters, and the Lights range which includes Digestives, Rich Tea, HobNobs and Milk Chocolate Digestives – all 30 % lower in fat than the standard variants.

Both traditional favourites like Rich Tea and Digestives, and new ranges, will continue to ensure generations enjoy the great taste of McVitie's biscuits!

Source: www.unitedbiscuits.co.uk (Stand: 11.09.2011)

Here is McVitie's briefing:

Client:	United Biscuits, a major British manufacturer of chocolates and biscuits. McVitie's is one of their 18 brands
Product:	McVitie's Hob Nobs, a roll of biscuits available in three varieties: plain chocolate, milk chocolate and plain
Target Market:	Primarily young people, age group 14–29
Competitors:	All major German sweets manufacturers, especially Leibniz and Bahlsen
Promise:	Healthy and tasty
Features:	HobNobs are wholemeal biscuits. The original biscuit made from rolled oats, wholemeal, sugar & vegetable oil. Packed in a cannister with resealable lid
UK slogan:	'One nibble and your're nobbled'
Tone:	Funny but not laughable

Promoting a new magazine – Launch event and press release

Task 1

A pitch meeting

In event management, deciding on an agency works in the same way as described above in the case of an advertising agency (pages 95). When a company or corporation decides to work with an external partner, for example to create and realise a special event, it usually contacts different event agencies, provides them with a briefing and invites them to present their ideas in a pitch-meeting. Then the most creative and/or most reasonable concept is usually picked and the corresponding agency gets the contract.

In order to create a real situation, split up into groups of four with each group representing an event agency.

Prepare a presentation by using all media available (posters, transparencies, board etc.). Your preparation time is 50 minutes and the actual presentation should not be longer than 10 minutes.

As a class listen attentively to the different presentations and take notes in order to decide on the best concept. Be prepared to have reasons for your decision.

Situation
The German publisher Gruner + Jahr AG & Co. KG intends to launch an English version of their German magazine "GEO" on the British market. The company wants to celebrate the launch in London together with 350 guests from society, politics, media and science.

Task
Suggest a location and develop a concept for the event. Create an event that stays on people's minds and helps the GEO magazine to an exceptional start in Britain.

The following websites might help you to get additional information and ideas:

www.guj.de
www.geo.de
www.gujmedia.de
www.londontown.com

Client:	Gruner + Jahr AG & Co. KG, Europe's largest magazine publisher.
Product:	GEO is a general-interest feature magazine and has been edited in Germany since 1976. Circulation: about 550,000 frequency: monthly
Target Market:	Primarily well-educated people, higher income, age group 20–50
Competitors:	None
Promise:	Innovative, journalistic quality and competence

Info Point

If you need support in preparing your presentation, turn to unit 5 on meetings (page 99) and the corresponding skill file (page 143) to be able to deliver a professional presentation.

Task 2

A press release

Situation

The event is over and was a real success. Now Gruner + Jahr asks you to draft a press release in order to inform the press. It should focus on the event mainly but also refer to the new magazine. Target groups are regional media and general interest magazines.

Task

Write a press release according to the format presented above (page 83–84).

Meetings and presentations

5

Kick-off: Preparing, chairing and attending international meetings and writing reports

Meetings are an essential part of business life. They are used to collect and share information, make announcements, discuss issues, solve problems, build relationships, brainstorm ideas and, perhaps most importantly, make decisions. Chairing or participating in meetings requires a range of skills, including the ability to lead, facilitate and arbitrate. When preparing, chairing or participating in a meeting, you should consider aspects such as planning, getting started, discussion management and decision-making/closing.

Task 1

Discuss your experience in class:
In the office, …

- … what kind of meetings do you usually attend?
- … what is usually discussed there?
- … are they formal or informal?
- … do you have to prepare meetings?
- … do you have to take over tasks as an attendant of a meeting?

Aims

You learn ...
... how to plan and prepare a meeting.
... how to deal with procedural matters.
... how to set up an agenda.
... how to take the minutes of a meeting.
... how to chair a meeting.
... how to give a presentation.
... how to present statistics.
... how to write a report.

Topics

Topic 1: Planning and preparing a meeting

Planning a meeting includes good scheduling, setting up an agenda and also planning your language. Preparation also depends on the kind of meeting.

Task 1

Which things should you take care of when planning a meeting from the preparational and organisational side?
Preparing a meeting:

- invite participants
- ...

The same procedure as last time?

Task 2

No matter what kind of meeting – a weekly gathering in the office to discuss the projects' status, a committee meeting or the Annual General Meeting – it usually follows the same procedure.
What kind of procedure can you imagine?

- Greeting the attendees
- Introducing oneself
- ...
- ...
- ...

Topic 2: Setting up an agenda

Before a meeting, an agenda has to be set up containing the items of business that have to be discussed. This agenda should be distributed to all participants of the meeting beforehand so that everybody can prepare for the meeting. Often the chairperson also sends out an e-mail in advance asking for items that the participants wish to be included in the agenda.

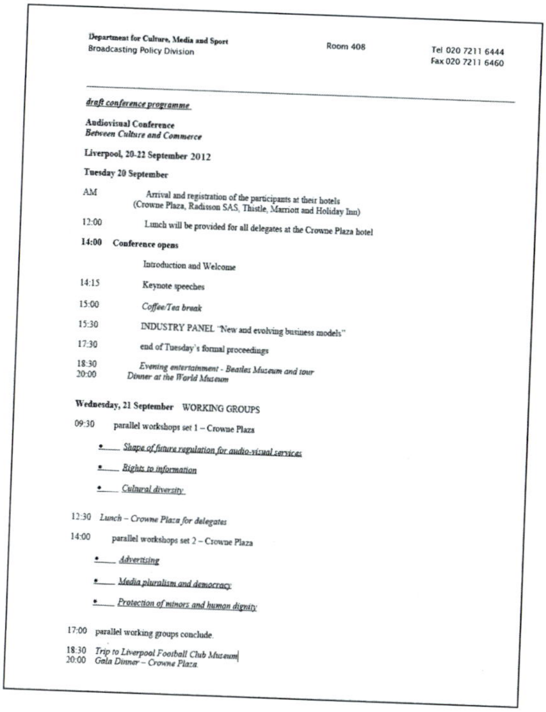
Department for Culture, Media and Sport
Broadcasting Policy Division
Room 408
Tel 020 7211 6444
Fax 020 7211 6460

draft conference programme

Audiovisual Conference
Between Culture and Commerce

Liverpool, 20-22 September 2012

Tuesday 20 September

AM	Arrival and registration of the participants at their hotels (Crowne Plaza, Radisson SAS, Thistle, Marriott and Holiday Inn)
12:00	Lunch will be provided for all delegates at the Crowne Plaza hotel
14:00	**Conference opens**
	Introduction and Welcome
14:15	Keynote speeches
15:00	*Coffee/Tea break*
15:30	INDUSTRY PANEL "New and evolving business models"
17:30	end of Tuesday's formal proceedings
18:30	*Evening entertainment - Beatles Museum and tour*
20:00	*Dinner at the World Museum*

Wednesday, 21 September WORKING GROUPS

09:30	parallel workshops set 1 – Crowne Plaza
	• *Shape of future regulation for audio-visual services*
	• *Rights to information*
	• *Cultural diversity*
12:30	*Lunch – Crowne Plaza for delegates*
14:00	parallel workshops set 2 – Crowne Plaza
	• *Advertising*
	• *Media pluralism and democracy*
	• *Protection of minors and human dignity*
17:00	parallel working groups conclude.
18:30	*Trip to Liverpool Football Club Museum*
20:00	*Gala Dinner – Crowne Plaza*

Task 1

List items which should appear in a good agenda:

- Venue, time, date
- ...
- ...
- ...

5 Unit

Expression Bank

Agenda

- Has everyone received a copy of the agenda?
- Would anybody wish to add another point to our agenda?
- I'd like to add an item to the agenda.
- I'd like to put another item on the agenda.
- Could we delete item 5 from the agenda?
- We've got a full agenda.

Task 2

Have you ever attended a meeting with **people you don't know** or with **colleagues you haven't met for a while**? How do you usually approach them in such a situation?

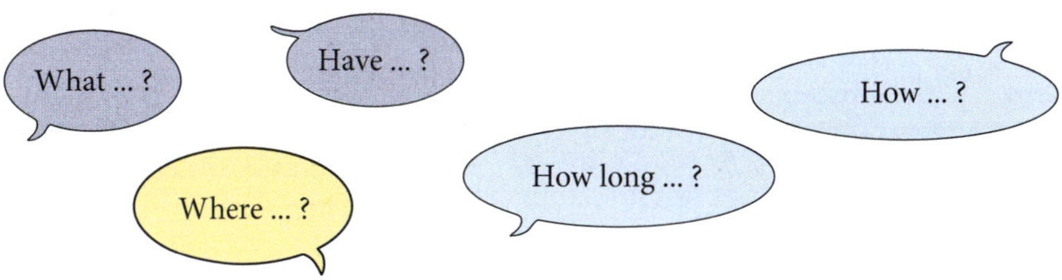

Task 3

Imagine you are engaging in conversations at a conference welcome party.

1. Write one question for each word given on page 101 suitable for first meetings at such an occasion. Remember the two different target groups (see page 146–147).
2. Role-play an informal pre-meeting conversation together with your partner using these questions.

Info Point

Similar to telephoning, on occasions such as meetings, conferences etc. small talk is used to create a friendly atmosphere between conversation partners. Have a look at the skill file for small talk to avoid any pitfalls. It is also important to know when and how to change from chatting to business (pages 145).

Task 4

"A meeting is an event where people keep minutes and lose hours"
What does this quote express about the time and quality of a meeting?
Have you ever taken the minutes of a meeting? What are your experiences?

Topic 3: Taking the minutes

The minutes are the official notes taken during a meeting summarising what is talked about and the decisions made. They are usually circulated to the participants afterwards and confirmed at the beginning of the following meeting if the participants are identical. They then approve them and the chairperson confirms them officially by signing them.
In general they should be a summary of the main decisions. A short description of arguments is alright but they should not include all arguments for and against particular suggestions.

Task

Layout of the minutes
Londonposters.com, a company for advertising media, is having an ordinary formal meeting to discuss the development of their innovation of posters with 3D, their so called "LivingPosterPeople". Please arrange the following items in the correct sequence to produce a professional layout of the minutes.

Londonposters.com

1. Matters arising
   Ms Miller asked about the new launch date of the new campaign to promote LivingPosterPeople to interested companies. Dr Hunt confirmed that it was to be kept, but that the PR agency had not yet started to draft the respective press release.
2. Dr Hunt proposed to intensify the cooperation with the London Chamber of Commerce. They should be approached in order to deliver a presentation of the innovation and concept at their next house fair in order to reach other members as potential customers.
3. After considerable discussion it was approved in principle by a vote of four in favour and one against this project.
4. Minutes of the third ordinary meeting
   of the team of posters with 3D
   on Tuesday, March 27, 2012 at 8.30 am
   in Conference Room A, first floor, Byatt Building,
   12 Covent Garden, London
5. Ms Miller reported that the sales department had distributed a mailing to existing customers in order to use them as multipliers for this new means of communication with the target groups.
6. Present: Ms Anne Cook - chairperson
   Mr John Brown
   Ms Jill Miller
   Dr Peter Hunt
   Mr Richard Sand
7. Minutes of the previous meeting
   The chairperson confirmed the minutes of the second meeting as there were no amendments.
8. Mr Sand was asked to contact the London Chamber of Commerce in order to fix an appointment. He also agreed to prepare the necessary material.
9. The chairperson opened the meeting at 8.35 am.
10. Date of the next meeting
    The secretary will inform the participants of the date and time of the next meeting, which will be held in the second week of April.
    As there was no further business, the chairperson closed the meeting at 9.30 am.
11. Apologies for absence
    Ms Judy Print was unable to attend.
12. Report on the development of LivingPosterPeople
    Mr Brown informed the meeting on the order status of LivingPosterPeople. So far fifteen companies, all in the larger London area, have booked spaces for posters with 3D for a timespan of six months.
13. ______________________ ______________
    Confirmed by Ms Anne Cook Date
    Chairperson

Unit 5

5
Unit

Info Point

If an item appears on the agenda it must also appear in the minutes even if it is not discussed in the meeting.

e. g. "Apologies for absence" or "Matters arising"
No participant was absent. There were no matters arising.

Expression Bank

Minutes

- Has everyone seen the minutes?
- Has everybody got a copy of the minutes of our last meeting?
- Can we take the minutes as read?
- Who is going to take/keep the minutes?
- John has volunteered to keep the minutes. Thank you, John.
- Ms Point is not present (excused).
- First/second etc. point/item on the agenda
- Miscellaneous

Language of the minutes

The language of minutes is usually formal in style. The writer of the minutes refers to himself or herself as secretary whereas all other participants are designated by their title and surname. The content of the meeting as it appears in the minutes is given in reported speech.

The use of tense and voice

The simple past tense of the verb is used to describe what happened at a meeting: e. g. Anne Cook **chaired** the meeting.
The past perfect tense of the verb is used to relate to what happened before the meeting:
e. g. Fifteen companies **had booked** spaces for posters with 3D.
Both, the active and passive voice can be used:
e. g. **active:** Anne Cook **confirmed** the minutes.
passive: The minutes **were confirmed** by Anne Cook.

Direct speech (meeting)	Reported speech (minutes)
Ms Miller: "When **will** be the new launch date?"	Ms Miller asked when the new launch date **would** be.
Dr Hunt: "**Has** the London Chamber of Commerce been contacted about the cooperation?"	Dr Hunt asked whether the London Chamber of Commerce **had** been contacted about the cooperation.

Ms Cook: "Other companies **may** be interested in LivingPosterPeople.	Ms Cook said that other companies **might** be interested in Living PosterPeople."
Mr Brown: "**I** will contact the London Chamber of Commerce."	Mr Brown agreed that **he** would contact the London Chamber of Commerce.
Mr Sand: "**We** should contact other companies."	Mr Sand suggested that **the committee** should contact other companies.
Ms Cook: "I put together a list of companies **yesterday**."	Ms Cook explained that she had put together a list of companies **the day before.**
Dr Hunt: "Then you should start calling them **tomorrow**."	Dr Hunt advised the committee calling them **the next day.**

Info Point

Practice writing the minutes occasionally by keeping track of what's happening in class. It's also a good way to keep the people missing a class informed about what has been happening.

Info Point

In the media sector minutes are often taken in a less formal way and can have the shape of so-called time and action plans. They are usually tables or excelsheets with columns indicating who does what and when, with a separate column for the status of this activity.

Who	What	When	Status

Topic 4: Chairing a meeting

A meeting can be seen from the chairperson's or from the participants' perspective. Each function involves specific tasks and corresponding behaviour. The following example looks at the chairperson's job accompanied by additional information and the phrases which are necessary to fulfil the task.

Steps	Additional Information	Phrases[1]
1. Opening the meeting.	The chairperson opens the meeting. In order to get out of the daily routine and get the tone right, it might be recommendable to start the meeting with an ice-breaker, for example a question, a joke or a quiz or simple questions such as asking participants to outline three things they expect from the meeting.	• Right, I think we should make a start. • Let's get down to business, shall we? • Good morning/afternoon everyone. • Welcome everybody. • Thank you very much for coming today.
2. Introducing visitors and explaining absences.	As a matter of politeness visitors and absent participants should be mentioned.	• First, I'd like to introduce a colleague from our Paris office. Would you like to say a few words about yourself? • Anne apologises for not being here today. She's with a customer. • Tim has been delayed. He should be here in about fifteen minutes.
3. Confirming the minutes of the previous meeting and identifying a person for the new minutes	Usually the minutes of the previous meeting have been circulated before the next meeting in order for every participant to check their correctness. If not, they are read out again. They are then amended or accepted as read. A new participant has to be identified to take the minutes of the present meeting, or, ideally, should be identified prior to the meeting in order to avoid reluctance.	• Has everyone seen the minutes? • Can we take the minutes as read? • Jane, would you mind taking the minutes today?

[1] Compare: Expression Bank "Minutes" on page 104.

Steps	Additional Information	Phrases[1]
4. Explaining the reason for the meeting and structuring it	The chairperson has to make sure that everyone knows the purpose of the meeting and has a copy of the agenda. He is also responsible for keeping the time that has been allocated to the meeting.	• Has everyone received/got a copy of the agenda? • The purpose of today's meeting is to discuss our new marketing campaign. • Now, let's look at the agenda in detail. • We've planned a maximum of one hour for the meeting. Therefore, we'll finish at 10 o'clock at the latest. • First, Peter will give us a short presentation of the results of last year's marketing campaign. Then, Jane will inform us about the latest status. After that, we will have a short discussion before deciding what to do this year.
5. Keeping the thread and discipline	The chairperson should also take care of preventing participants from digressing. If they do he has to remind them to return to the business at hand.	• I'm afraid we're moving too far away from the subject. • We're beginning to lose sight of the main point. The question is ... • Could you stick to the subject/keep to the point, please. • Let's not get side-tracked. The issue under discussion is ... • There seems to be a slight misunderstanding. • We cannot speak all at once. James, would you like to speak first? Then Gina. • We're running out of time, I'm afraid, so I must ask you to be brief. • Thank you, Peter. I think, we've all got the point now. Shall we move on?

[1] Compare: Expression Bank "Minutes" on page 104.

Steps	Additional Information	Phrases[1]
6. Keeping time	The chairperson's most important job is to keep the meeting moving in order not to lose time between agenda items.	• Is there anything to add before we move on to the next item on the agenda? • Could we move on to item two on the agenda? • Let's move on to item four: Last year's marketing campaign.
7. Summarising and taking a vote	In order to keep the thread and the timing it helps if the chairperson summarises the main points. If a decision has to be made it can be done by voting.	• Let me summarise the main decisions. • To sum up, we've decided to start a new marketing campaign next year. • Alright, let's put that to a vote. • Could we have a show of hands? Who's in favour of the proposal? Who's against? Any abstentions? • Would anyone like to propose a motion on this point? • Would anyone like to second the motion? • The motion is carried. • The motion has been rejected by six votes to four.
8. Postponing a decision	In the case that a decision cannot be reached, the chairperson can postpone it.	• I think we should postpone this decision until we have further information. • I suggest that we take a final decision on this at our next meeting.
9. Closing the meeting	After the main items on the agenda have been covered, the chairperson checks whether there is any other business and then closes the meeting.	• Is there any other business? • Are there any other points to be raised? • Thank you all very much for your contributions. • OK, that's it for today. See you all again on Friday.

Task

Listen to the following recording of a meeting. Complete the transcript with suitable expressions you have learnt.

[1] Compare: Expression Bank "Minutes" on page 104.

CP: Good morning, Ladies and Gentlemen. I am chairing today's meeting about our marketing activities for "Blackberry" and I ______________ ______________ today. First of all I would like to ______________ for today which is Jane English from our office in London.

Jane, ______________?

JE: Yes, thank you, Peter. My ______________, I ______________ and I have been working for "Marketing & More" for a year now. Starting off in the public relations department, I am now working for the event manager Jenny Wilson in the event department, I have been invited to attend this meeting in order to report about our marketing activities for our main client "Blackberry" for whom we are currently organising the event "Mobile World" in London.

CP: Thank you, Jane. Unfortunately, Mr Roberts and Ms Jones ______________ ______________ as they are attending a press conference for "Blackberry" in Berlin. Mr Miller ______________ ______________. Now, ______________, shall we? Jill ______________. Thank you Jill. Now, let's ______________. The purpose of today's meeting is to discuss the marketing activities for "Blackberry" for the following quarters. First, ______________ ______________ of the results of last year's marketing activities. ______________, Jane will inform us about the latest status. ______________ ______________, we will have a short discussion before deciding what to do this year.

CP: We cannot speak all at once. ______________? Then Jill.

PM: What we haven't discussed at all so far: how are we going to go about doing the advertising campaign?

CP: ______________. The issues under discussion are the marketing activities in general. We cannot discuss any specific advertising strategy unless we know how much budget is planned for advertising. Jill, ______________, I'm afraid, so I must ask you to be brief.

JB: I think that we should repeat last year's successful activities and only alter them in the cases where it went completely wrong such as with the TV spot and the Covent Garden event. We know the weaknesses there and can alter the strategy accordingly.

CP: ______________: We've decided to take over last year's campaign and to add new ideas at the crucial points. I would like to put that to the vote. ______________? Who's in favour of the proposal? Who's against? ______________? Fine, everybody is in favour. So I thank you all for your contributions and I will see you all again next Monday.

Topic 5: Writing reports

Info Point

Often the minutes of a meeting are also referred to as meeting report. The following excercises about linking language and writing objectively are also important for the writing of the minutes. The other aspects of this unit refer to a report as it is described below.

"Your 200-pages-report was not too clear - I axed it down to 20 lines."

In your working life you can often be involved in situations where you have to solve problems, make decisions and find new strategies in order to further develop the company you are working for or help your client to put his ideas into practice.
A report is a helpful tool to gather information, analyse a situation and develop strategies. At some point you may be in the situation to have to write a report yourself.
In general, there are many different kinds of reports – a meeting report, a technical research paper, a market analysis, a marketing debrief, a staff appraisal or a chairman's speech to name just a few. These examples have very different formats depending on the respective target group and objective. Before deciding on the format, it is therefore vitally important to ask yourself who your readers are and what you want to achieve with the report.

Info Point

Similar to giving a presentation, the objective and the target group are the most important things to consider when planning a report. It's them on which the format depends. As the respective questions resemble the presentation, have a look at the skill file on presentations and reports (pages 143).

How to structure a report

When you are writing a meeting report there are different ways to structure it. The most common basic structure is

1. Objective
2. Background information
3. Main issues (detailed)
4. Options with advantages and disadvantages
5. Recommendations or solutions and conclusions

Task 1

Within that structure it is important to also present your information in a structured way. Compare the two paragraphs below. Which one do you prefer and why?

1. Last year produced excellent results for Penguin audiobooks. The launch was a success and subsequently our turnover increased by 40 percent in that section. First we started with a small edition of four different audiobooks with 10 000 pieces of each. There was an enormous demand and they were sold out soon. Then we increased the edition up to 50 000 pieces of each and also started to export them to the rest of Europe. By now we also have demand in the US and are planning to expand our range.
2. The launch of Penguin audiobooks last year was a success and subsequently our turnover increased by 40 percent in that section. First we started with a small edition of four different audiobooks with 10 000 pieces of each. There was an enormous demand and they were sold out soon. Then we increased the edition up to 50 000 pieces of each and also started to export them to the rest of Europe. By now we also have demand in the US and are planning to expand our range. Altogether Penguin audiobooks produced excellent results last year.

Linking language

The structure of a report as it is described above goes down to the level of content. The way it is linked together decides on the transparency of the message you try to bring across. This can be achieved by using specific expressions which help to link together sentences and paragraphs such as “accordingly”, “moreover”, “therefore” and “as a result” to name a few.

Task 2

Have a look at the following sentences and bring them in the right order by identifying linking language.
The rise of bookingartists.com

1. The reason for the success of bookingartists.com was the launch of a new user-friendly software.
2. Indeed, the company now has a big number of clients that keep returning.
3. Bookingartists.com can look back on a very successful year 2011.
4. Moreover, the number of page impressions rose by nearly 40 percent.
5. Despite the difficult situation on the market, the company overtook its competitor “Booking Today” and became market leader.

Info Point

The skill file on presentation and reports gives you further examples of linking language (page 145).

Topic 6: Giving a presentation

Task 1

Often presentations are part of meetings and often they can be very boring.
If you want your presentation to be a success and not have your audience yawn away what would you have to take care of?

- … topic – What are you talking about?
- …
- …
- …
- …

Task 2

Your strengths and weaknesses as a presenter

Do you know about your strengths and weaknesses when giving a presentation?

- Get together in groups of four.
- Pick one of the topics below (each of you).
- Prepare and give a short presentation to your group members.
- Give each other feedback on how you came across as a presenter.

Topics

1. A general introduction to your company.
2. An introduction to the organisational structure of your company.
3. A new product or service being offered by your company.
4. A summary of training opportunities within your company.

Task 3

Structuring your presentation

a) *What do you know about the structure of a presentation?*
What are the main points?
Listen to the following presentation and try to identify the main structuring points.
Are there any you have not yet considered?

b) *Practice introducing yourself and your topic by choosing one of the topics below.*
There you'll also find the corresponding words you need for the introduction.
Example: "Good afternoon everybody, my name is Annette Bauer. I work in the marketing department of Tesco's and with today's presentation, I would like to give you an insight into our company's customer service. I will first focus on the change of customer needs, secondly I'll take a look at our range of service activies and lastly I'll conclude with the changes in our service policy. If you have any questions, please don't hesitate to interrupt me".

Company: **BBC World Service**

Topic: Learning English from the Internet

Launch of new service on www.bbc.co.uk/worldservice/learningenglish/

Product features

Advertising concept

Company: **Penguin UK**

Topic: Celebration of 70th birthday

Launch of audiobook series

Author events all over the country

Publishing of 70 new Penguin pockets

More information on www.penguin.co.uk

Company: **British Council**

Topic: Promoting their study programme

Encourage young people to come to Britain to study or take language exams

Marketing concept

More information on www.britishcouncil.org/new/

Company: **Times Newspapers Ltd**

Topic: Gaining new subscribers for the ePaper www.thetimes.co.uk/tto/news/

Expansion into the European Market by attracting new subscribers especially from Germany and France

Benefits

Communication concept

When giving a presentation it is important to structure it in such a way that the audience always knows what you are referring to at that moment. You can find suitable phrases in the following Expression Banks.

Expression Bank

Introduction

- Good morning, ladies and gentlemen.
- It's a pleasure to welcome you to …
- Let me introduce myself. My name is …
- I'm the marketing manager of …
- I work for Marketing & More …
- Today's topic is the new marketing campaign for "Harrods Events" for the upcoming quarter.
- What I'd like to present to you today is …
- I'm going to focus on the following items …
- Firstly …, secondly …, thirdly …
- My first point is …, then …, at last …
- I'll start out with …, then I'll move on to …, and I'll end with …

Main part

- I'd now like to turn to my first major point.
- So much for the first point.
- This is all I have to say about …
- Having covered this final point, I'm now approaching the end of my presentation.
- This brings me to the end of my presentation.
- In a nutshell …
- Let me briefly summarise the major issues.
- To make a long story short …

Ending

- As I read the facts and figures …
- I'm convinced …
- What does this all mean for us?
- Are there any questions?
- Thank you for your attention.

Info Point

You will find further information on the vocabulary of presenting in the skill file for giving presentations (pages 143).

Topic 7: Presenting statistics

Unit 5

Task 1

Often, statistics are part of a presentation. As the description of trends and developments needs special vocabulary, check how many of the words below you can allocate to the graphs.

to pick up, to stabilise, to skyrocket, to go up, to level off, to flatten out, to go down, to grow, to remain stable, to fluctuate, to decrease, to decline, to stay at the same level, to drop, to slump, to reach a minimum/low/low-point, to increase, to soar, to shoot up, to rise, to fall, to recover, to remain steady, to hit a low, to plummet, to oscillate, to recuperate, to reach a peak/maximum/high/ high-point

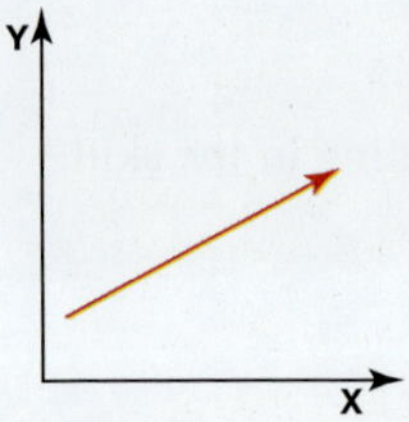

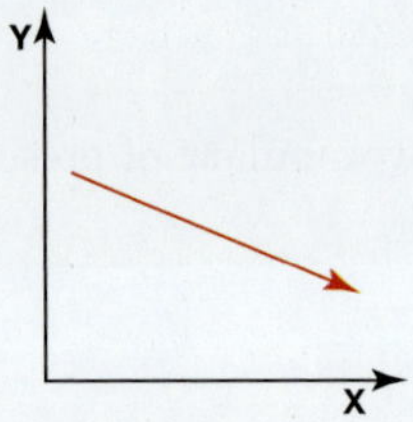

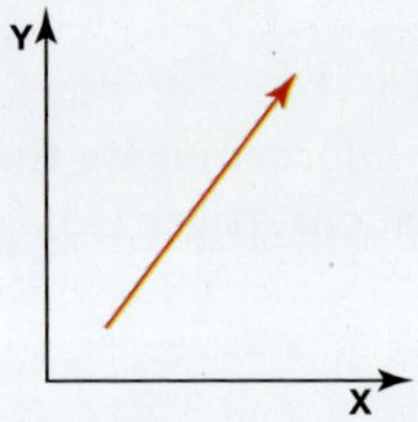

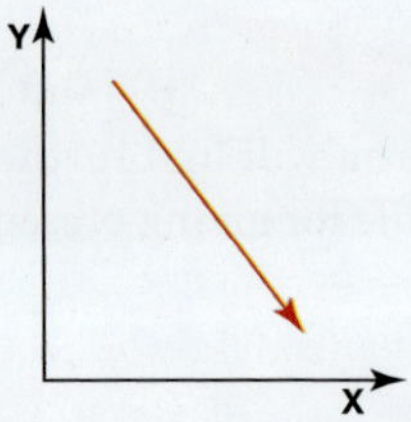

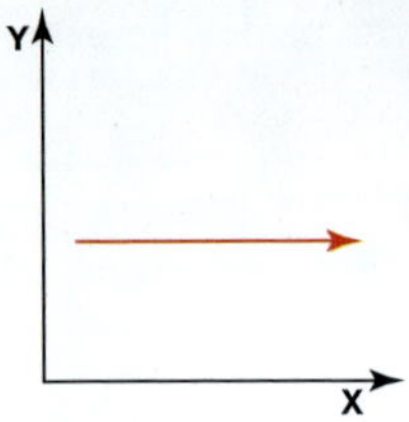

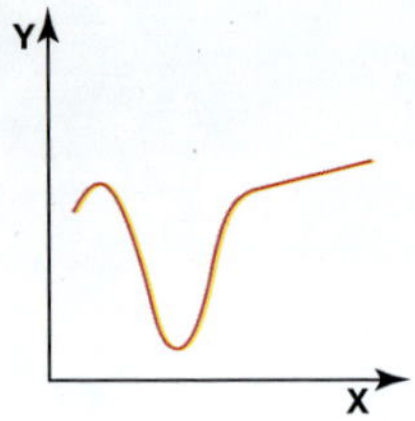

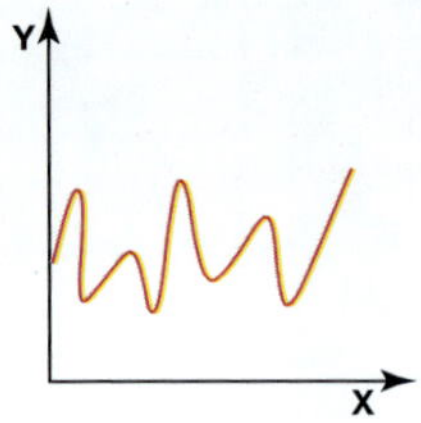

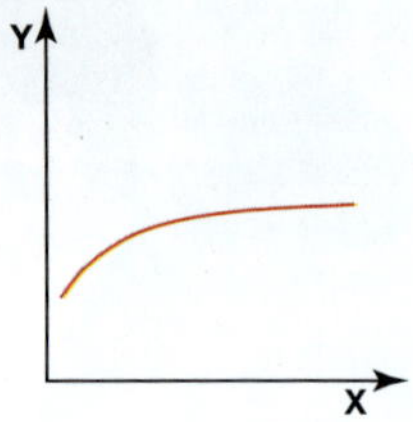

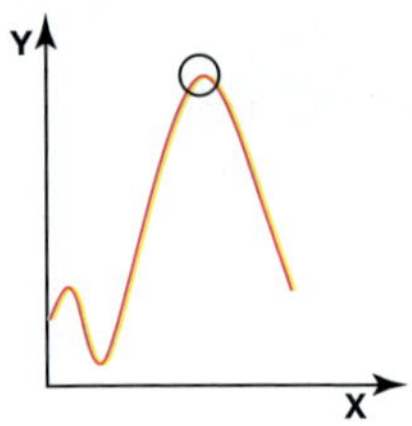

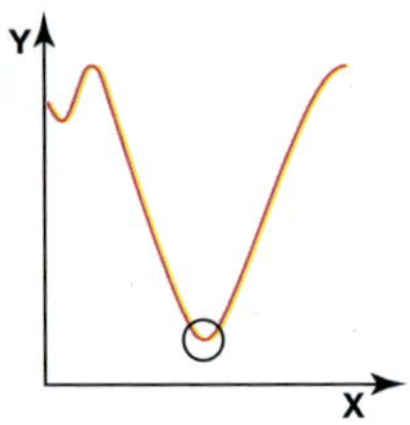

Task 2

Below you find descriptions of economic developments. Draw the graphs according to the descriptions.

1. Our agency's turnover **increased dramatically** last year, before it **levelled off** due to the loss of two strong clients.
2. The fluctuation of staff **reached a peak** in 2006, **oscillating** for a year before **diminishing** to nearly zero in 2011.

3. The sale of the new pocket series **soared** after its authors had toured the country. It is likely **to decrease** and **reach a minimum** in the course of this year before it **picks up** again at the beginning of next year.
4. The number of companies deciding to attend trade fairs is going **down** continuously due to the related costs and the receding number of visitors. It is expected to **reach a minimum** in 2011 and to have **flattened out** by 2015.
5. The consumers' awareness of the new advertising campaign **shot up** to 100 percent and has **levelled off** there since.

Getting the tense right – Using adjectives and adverbs

When you describe statistics, apart from using the correct vocabulary you also have to pay attention to the correct tense depending on whether you describe developments in the present, past or future. Additionally, you can also be more precise in your description by using corresponding adjectives/adverbs.

Tense	**Refers to a fact which …**	**Example**
Simple present	is always true	Companies do not organise big events when they are short of money.
Present continuous	is true at this moment	Turnover is rising.
Simple past	was true in the past (specified time)	Turnover rose last year.
Present perfect	was true in the past and is still true now	Turnover has risen.
Future	will happen in the future	Turnover will rise.

Adjectives and adverbs	
To show short, quick or unexpected changes	sudden/ly, sharp/ly, abrupt/ly, rapid/ly
To show small but important changes	significant/ly, marked/ly
To show large, important changes	substantial/ly, steep/ly
To show small changes	bare/ly, slow/ly, slight/ly, moderate/ly
To show slow, long changes	gradual/ly, general/ly, steady / steadily
To show short-lasting changes	short-lived, brief/ly

Task 3

1. Write down five job-related sentences and dictate them to your neighbour.
2. Draw the graphs belonging to the sentences your neighbour dictated to you.

Task 4

Presentation exercise

1. Look at the two graphs below. Choose one of them and find a topic for it denominating the x- and y-axes.
2. Prepare a three-minute presentation on the graph of your choice. Make sure that your presentation has a proper introduction, main part and ending.
3. Practise your presentation with a partner.
4. Give your presentation in front of class.

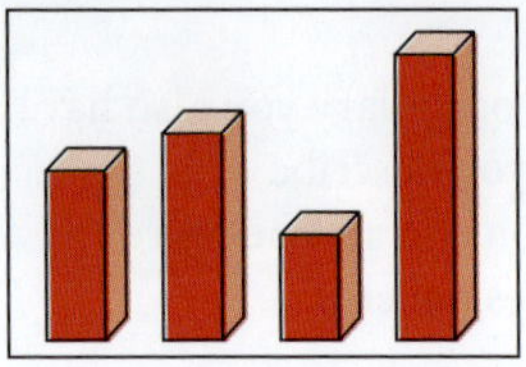

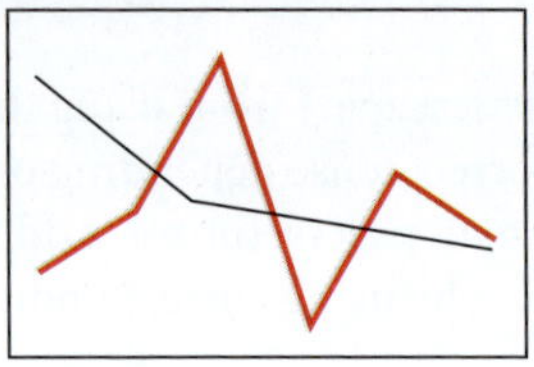

An appointments commitee meeting

Your company's job advertisement has attracted many applicants (compare unit 6, pages 121). The management has decided on four candidates and invited them for a job interview. Together with your team, you have to choose one of them to become the new team member. In order to do so you will receive information on the potential candidates from your teacher. Then there will be an appointments committee meeting where you are to present your views and in the end propose a candidate.

Task

Devide your class into equal groups (of ideally seven people) all representing meeting participants.

In each group there will be a representative of one of the following (for details see rolecard that you will be given by your teacher):

- human resources department
- team leader
- team specific colleague
- apprentice in the team
- women's representative
- top management

Additionally: A chairperson

Each of you works through the four candidates' documents her/himself and decides on the person who – from your point view (according to role) – is best suited for the job.

In the end two groups are to perform the appointments committee meeting by following the agenda below. The other two groups function as consultants and observe the actual performance in order to give feedback on how the discussion moves and the final decision is made.

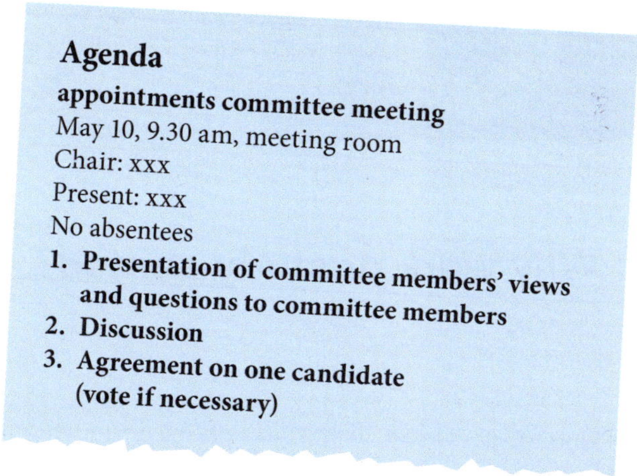

Agenda

appointments committee meeting
May 10, 9.30 am, meeting room
Chair: xxx
Present: xxx
No absentees

1. **Presentation of committee members' views and questions to committee members**
2. **Discussion**
3. **Agreement on one candidate (vote if necessary)**

A job abroad

6

Kick-off: Why work or study abroad?

Task 1

Work with a partner. Ask each other about your working or studying experience in foreign countries.

- Find out about his/her jobs/fields of study, about his/her likes and dislikes and his/her recommendations to other students!
- If your interview partner has never been to a foreign country for studying or working purposes, ask him/her why not and whether he/she could imagine doing so in the future.

Task 2

Now have a look at the table below.

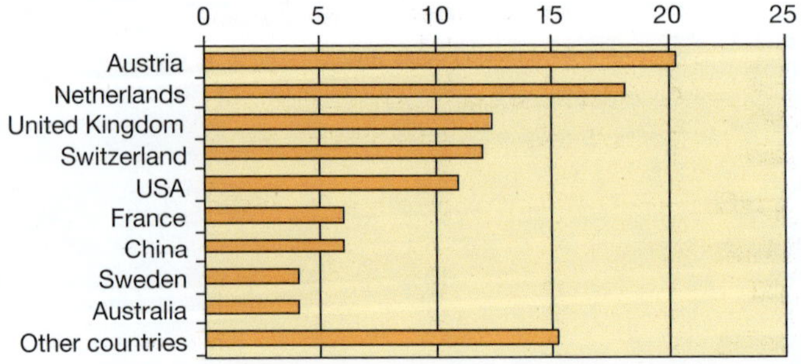

Top destinations for German students studying abroad in 2009 (in %).
Quelle: Eigene Darstellung mit Daten des Statistischen Bundesamtes

Answer the following questions:

- What do you think are the reasons for the different attitudes towards the countries?
- Find an explanation why Austria, the Netherlands and the United Kingdom are so high on the list.
- In which country would you like to study/work? Where not? Give reasons.

Aims

You learn ...
... how to read and analyse job advertisements
... how to write CVs and cover letters for your job application
... how to prepare for and conduct a job interview

Topics

Topic 1: Understanding job advertisements and contacting companies

When roaming through job ads in a newspaper or the internet, you will most probably come across a lot of job titles, skills and other job-related words which you are not familiar with. The two exercises below should help you learn to understand job ads in English.

Task 1

Have a look at the selection of job ads.

a) *Explain the kind of job the employer is offering and the tasks the future employee will have to fulfil.*

b) *List all the skills and qualifications required by the employers and explain what they mean.*

PR Account Manager
£25-£40k
Pricejamieson
Top 10 communications agency has an opening for a PR Account Manager in their Digital Media Division, focussing on financial services, corporate, b2b and consumer clients. You must have online-PR and marketing experience.

News International Newspapers Ltd
Administration Assistant

Salary: £16 000 p.a. Hours: 9am-5pm

A vacancy exists for an Administration Assistant to work for the Director of Retail Trade & Marketing.

Extremely varied duties including some secretarial assistance.

Candidates must have good organisational skills, an excellent telephone manner and the ability to work under pressure.

Info Point

The German Federal Institute for Professional Training (Bundesinstitut für Berufliche Bildung – BIBB) has issued an English translation for most of the training profiles, mostly by adding the word "clerk" to the field of work, so that „Medienkaufmann/-frau Digital und Print" becomes "publishing clerk", „Kaufmann/-frau für Marketingkommunikation" becomes "advertising clerk", „Veranstaltungskaufmann/-frau" "event manager" and „Kaufmann/-frau für audiovisuelle Medien" becomes "audiovisual media clerk".
However, most of these translations are not used in any English-speaking country for lack of a comparable training profile. You will have to help yourself with descriptions of what you do.
In job ads, you will find more specific job titles, such as "editor", "A&R representative" or "PR manager".

Task 2

Match the expressions on the left taken from job advertisements with their descriptions on the right.

1. skills	a) *ability to handle everything having to do with information technologies*
2. qualifications	b) *the talent to interact with other people, e.g. being a team player*
3. in-house function	c) *full domination of a foreign language*
4. spreadsheets	d) *event that takes place inside a company's premises*
5. IT-literacy	e) *part of a company that manages the staff, accounts, etc.*
6. soft skills	f) *discuss in order to reach an agreement, e.g. a contract*

7. fluency — g) *ability to do something expertly and well*
8. to negotiate — h) *used in order to calculate prices, developments, etc. with the help of a computer programme such as Excel*
9. administration — i) *abilities that can be testified by diplomas, degrees, etc.*

Info Point

Where to find job advertisements on the internet

US/Canada:	Great Britain/Ireland:	Australia/New Zealand
www.hoovers.com	www.fish4.co.uk	www.trademe.co.nz/jobs
www.rileyguide.com	http://jobs.guardian.co.uk	www.jobnet.com.au
www.collegegrad.com	www.planetrecruit.com	www.monster.com.au
www.monster.com	www.jobserve.com	www.jobsearch.gov.au
www.careerbuilder.com	www.careersoft.co.uk	
www.truecareers.com	www.jobsite.co.uk	
http://jobmarket.nytimes.com/	www.jobs.ie	

German institutions that offer internships, high school years, etc.:
www.cdc.de, www.daad.de, www.career-contact.de, www.praktikum-service.de

Task 3

Research these and other websites that offer jobs in your line of business.

Task 4

Calling your future employer
Often, before you take the next step of writing a job application as described in topics 2 and 3, it is advisable to call the company you want to apply to. Sometimes, the job ad specifically asks you to ring up before sending a letter of application. Especially when sending an exploratory application, i.e. an application that does not refer to a job advertisement, you can find out important details in a short phone call. You should ask whether there are any chances of being employed at all (some companies may have a freeze on recruitment), who you should send the application to and any further details that might be of interest to you.

Listen to the dialogue between an applicant and the personnel department. Then answer the following questions:

1. What does the applicant try to find out?
2. How does the applicant react to the questions asked by the personnel manager?
3. What could the applicant have done in order to prepare for the phone call?

Topic 2: Writing a curriculum vitae (CV)

When you have found a job ad that interests you and that matches your skills and qualifications, you will have to write a letter of application. This usually consists of two parts: the curriculum vitae (called résumé in American English) and the cover letter. The CV is the key to your success and should be written with utmost care. It does not suffice to write one CV and attach it to all the applications you ever write– it should be tailored to the particular job you are applying for. There are some tips on how to write a good CV after the Task.

Task 1

What do you think is important when writing a good CV? Gather your ideas in a list:

- limit it to a maximum of two pages – you do not need to state everything you have ever done in a CV
- …
- …

On top of these dos and don'ts there is another difficulty for foreign applicants: the problem of translating school types, academic titles and degrees, etc. into English. As with the job titles, there often are no one-to-one translations and you have to come up with a good description. Sometimes it is even recommendable to stick to the German name and write an English equivalent in brackets as in the following example:

1999–2012 Albert-Schweitzer-Gymnasium (equivalent to grammar school)
2012 Abitur (equivalent to A-levels)

Some school types can be translated into English and some universities even have English names (have a look at some websites of German universities). Here are some possible translations for school types and degrees:

German	British English	American English	general
Grundschule	primary school	elementary school	primary education
Hauptschule	–secondary modern school	–junior high school	
Realschule	–secondary school	–junior high school	secondary
Gymnasium	grammar school	high school	education
Gesamtschule	comprehensive school	high school	

(höhere) Berufsfachschule (HöHa)	–business /commercial college	–business school	
Berufsschule	–vocational school	–(business) college	further
Fachhochschule	university of applied sciences	–college	education
Universität	university	university	
Abitur	A-levels	high school diploma	
Realschulabschluss	GCSE (O-levels)	secondary school examination	
Fachhochschulreife			entrance qualification for a university of applied sciences

Task 2

The typical sections of a CV are *personal details*, *education*, *work experience*, *skills* and *interests*.
Discuss with a partner which details these sections should include and how they should be structured. Also discuss the CV on page 126 – how would you evaluate it as an employer?

Types of CVs

A CV can be written in *(reverse) chronological* order, in *functional* order or in a combination of those two, called *chrono-functional* or simply *combination* CV.

A *reverse choronolgical* CV lists all the schools and jobs in a chronological order, starting with the most recent. The sample CV on page 126 is a reverse chronological one.
The *functional* CV does not list the educational and professional data in chronological order, but sorts them into different thematic groups.
A *combination* CV combines these two forms by listing work experience in chronological order while focussing on achievements and responsibilities in the functional part.

Sample CV

	Maria Brauckmann Holstätter Str. 64 52062 Aachen GERMANY (+49) 241 689452	
PERSONAL DATA	*Date of birth:*	27.08.1990
	Place of birth:	Heidelberg, Germany
	Marital status:	single
OBJECTIVE	An entry-level position in the film industry.	
EDUCATION	*RWTH Aachen* (University). Bachelor of Science degree in Marketing to be completed in May 2013. Courses include International Marketing, Marketing Research, Business Communications, Statistics and Computer Programming. *St. Albert Gesamtschule* (comprehensive school), 2000–2008. Abitur (A-levels) in business studies, Spanish and mathematics.	
RELATED EXPERIENCE	*Universidad de Salamanca*, Spain, Summer 2011. Comprehensive study of Spanish language and culture. Thorough analysis of political and economic system as well as the Spanish media. *Direct Marketing Competition, London University* – Winter Term 2010. Participated on student-team project to create direct marketing campaign for MTV. Gained practical experience in developing marketing report.	
WORK EXPERIENCE	*Musikkantine* (music store), Erftstadt, Summer 2012. Sales associate. Assisted in layout of store merchandise, stocking and quality control of inventory and operated cash register. Evaluated and presented recommendations for changes in store displays.	
SPECIAL SKILLS	*Typing/Word Processing:* 50 WPM	
	Computer:	Windows 7, database and presentation software
	Languages:	English (excellent working knowledge) Spanish (basic knowledge) German (native speaker)
PERSONAL INTERESTS	Enjoy volleyball, horseback riding, reading fiction, and playing chess.	
REFERENCES	Available upon request.	

Info Point

A job application in English-speaking countries is much shorter than a German one. It usually only includes the following and is not put into a folder:

- cover letter
- CV/résumé
- rarely: references, diplomas/reports (these will rather be presented upon request of the employer.)

As opposed to German applications, it is not common to send a photo particularly not in American ones. This has to do with the "equal-opportunities-policy" of these countries. Furthermore, most personal details (such as date and place of birth, marital status, religion, etc.) are omitted, unless you decide they are of advantage to your application.

Task 3

Discuss what the advantages and disadvantages of the three different types of CVs are. When would you choose which type?

Elements of a CV

Personal details often include only name, address, telephone numbers and other contact details such as e-mail. More personal details such as marital status, religion, etc. are usually not mentioned (see Info Point).

A career/job objective is mostly found in American CVs and contains a concise description of the applicant's aims concerning his professional career (e.g. "A challenging position as marketing manager at XY company").

Education: the description of your education should contain the name of schools/ universities with the corresponding city, period and degree (including an English translation or explanation). Only if your grades were very good, you should mention these. The more work experience you have, the less educational details should be mentioned; if you are a student you should give more details of your subjects, activities and thesis.

Work experience/employment history: this section includes the name and town of employers, periods of employment and positions held. Any achievements or accomplishments should be pointed out as these are synonyms for a successful career. Such achievements could be the innovation of a product, the management of a project or the responsibility for a certain budget. Whatever your achievements – use the action words in the box below in order to emphasise them.

Expression Bank

Action words – use these words to enhance your CV and to make it more powerful.

achieved	coordinated	evaluated	managed	produced
analysed	created	examined	minimised	promoted
attained	decided	expanded	modified	published
coached	designed	guided	motivated	recommended
collaborated	developed	improved	negotiated	researched
communicated	directed	increased	obtained	solved
consulted	eliminated	instructed	organised	studied
controlled	established	investigated	planned	trained

Qualifications/additional skills could be languages, computer skills or any extra courses you took. Do not forget to self-assess your skills, e.g. by writing "excellent skills of …" or "basic knowledge of …".

Personal interests are mentioned only when considered valuable for the job you are applying for or make you seem more interesting for the employer. Beside hobbies, personal interests can also include memberships in clubs or charitable associations.

Extracurricular activities are particularly important in the US If you are a student, you might want to mention any activities in politics, society or sports.

Publications are of particular interest for academic or journalistic professions – if you have published any books or articles, you should mention their title, date of publication and publisher.

Referees (BE)/References (AE): Different from German practice it is common in English-speaking countries to contact a referee (e.g. a former employer) instead of sending a certificate. Therefore you should write something like "references available upon request".

Task 4

Write your personal CV following the structure discussed above.

Topic 3: Writing a cover letter

The second important item which needs to be included in an application is the so-called cover letter. Here, you have to address the employer or personnel manager directly and give reasons for why you think you are the best for the job in question.

Task

Work in pairs. Imagine that you have received a lot of applications for a job in your company. Sort them into three piles: A – these look promising, B – these are possible candidates, C – hopeless cases.

1. I noted with interest your advertisement for a "PR Assistant" in today's Observer.
2. My name's Tom Parker and I can do great things for your company! I'm 28, unmarried, fit and healthy and I've got all the qualifications and experience to make me the ideal employee.
3. As you will see from my enclosed CV, I have been working for my present company for three years. I joined them as location manager and was promoted to production manager last year. Before that I had spent three years taking a full-time diploma course in media studies.
4. I wish to apply for the job you have advertised. Please send me further information.
5. I enclose a CV, which gives full details of my qualifications and work experience. In support of my application, I should like to mention the following points:
6. I am writing about the job in your advertisement in todays daily Mail. I am having four years experiance in the publishing trade as well as the qualificifications you required.
7. If you consider that my experience and qualifications are suitable, I would be available for interview at any time.
8. I am ambitious and my present job doesn't offer me the chance to expand.
9. I would be grateful if I could discuss the post available in person and perhaps go into my background and my suitability for the post in more detail.
10. Although my present employers are first-rate and our relationship is excellent, I am keen to extend my range and am looking for a more rewarding and challenging post.

What has been said above about CVs is also true for cover letters – make sure it refers to the particular job you are applying for. Also pay attention to the correct use of grammar, spelling and punctuation.

The **layout** of a cover letter is the same as of any formal letter – have a look at unit 2 for a sample layout.

The **structure** of your cover letter depends on whether you are answering a job advertisement or writing an exploratory letter, i.e. applying to a company that you are interested in, but that did not advertise any vacancies. Below you find a sample structure:

First paragraph: The first sentence must immediately get the employer's attention, even more so if you are not answering a job advertisement. If you are writing in answer to a job ad, you can refer to the position advertised, e.g. *"I am writing in response to your advertisement in last Saturday's edition of The Times"*. Furthermore, explain why your background makes you the best candidate for the position, e.g. *"Having completed my professional training as marketing assistant at*

In short:

Where did you hear/read about the job?
Why are you the best candidate?

Sample letter

Sarah Loosen
Jülicher Str. 76
52064 Aachen
Germany
Phone: +49-241-98657

Mr P. Appleton
Albion Publishing Ltd
45 Harbour Street
Newcastle NC6 34TG

October 25, 2012

Dear Mr Appleton,

I would like to apply for the position of Marketing Assistant to the Head of Marketing as advertised in "The Guardian" on Saturday, October 22, 2012. I am 23 years old and will soon be completing my professional training as publishing assistant at Wolf & Sohn publisher in Cologne. For three years I have been working in Wolf & Sohn's advertising, marketing and distribution departments. I was responsible for advertising sales and dealing with our subscribers. I have been actively involved in international marketing activities and speak fluent English and good French.

Albion publishers attracted my interest as a company dealing in both book and newspaper publishing. As an expert in newspaper publishing but with little experience in book publishing, working for Albion would be an interesting challenge for me. Furthermore, working in Great Britain will certainly broaden my horizon in both professional and personal respect.

Please find enclosed my CV showing qualifications and details of my work experience. I hope that my application is of interest to you. Naturally I would be prepared to come for an interview or a phone interview to start the selection process.

Yours sincerely,

Sarah Loosen
Sarah Loosen

Bertelsmann Music Group, I am confident that I would make a very successful PR assistant in your PR department."

Second paragraph: Detail what you could contribute to this company – show how this firm will benefit from your qualifications, e.g. *"In addition to my strong marketing background, I also offer significant experience in sales having worked in the sales department of BMG for six months. I am sure that my courses in customer relationship and presentation software would prove particularly useful in the position of a PR assistant."*

Which qualifications and experiences can you contribute to the company?

Third paragraph: Describe your interest in the company. Emphasise your knowledge of this firm and the industry in general, e.g. *"I am attracted to Musixx by your recent innovative expansion into niche markets. After studying different music labels, I have concluded that Musixx will be in a strong competitive position to benefit from upcoming changes in the industry."*

Why are you interested in this particular company?

Unit 6

Fourth paragraph: In the final paragraph, specifically request an interview. You may also include the hours when you can be reached, e.g. *"Naturally, I would welcome an interview to discuss the background I have outlined in the enclosed CV. I am best reached between 3 and 5 pm at +49-30-4738375."*

Request an interview.

Topic 4: Preparing for a job interview

If your application was successful, the recruiter will invite you to a job interview. A first interview might even be lead on the phone, especially if you applied from a foreign country and travelling to the company is quite expensive. Whatever the case, it is important to be well prepared.

Task 1

Cartoon
- Describe the situation in the cartoon.
- Why do you think the boss asked the applicant the question about the fox and the chickens?
- Can you explain the applicant's answer and the boss's reaction towards it?

Task 2

Remember what you did in order to prepare for your previous job interview(s). List at least five things that you would recommend to someone preparing for a job interview.

Task 3

Now remember some questions that you have been asked during an interview – German and English interviews are very similar in that respect. List at least one question for each of the categories mentioned below:
1. Questions regarding the applicant's personality
2. Questions regarding the applicant's education and work experience
3. Questions regarding the applicant's last job/employer
4. Questions regarding the company
5. Questions regarding working morale
6. Questions regarding the salary
7. Questions the applicant might ask

Task 4

Listen and discuss: Two job interviews

You will hear parts of two interviews. Then answer these questions:
1. Which of the candidates performed better? Why?
2. Which of the interviewers did the better job? Why?
3. What would you recommend the candidates and interviewers do in order to be more professional?

While listening a second time, write down the questions the interviewers ask and then decide which answer you would give to each of these questions.

Task 5

Roleplay: A job interview

Step 1: Choose five questions from the list you assembled in task 2 and answer these questions for yourself. Make some notes that you can use during the roleplay but avoid writing full sentences.

Step 2: Practise the job interview with a partner. Give him/her the questions you have chosen and answer them as freely and naturally as possible. Then switch roles.
Step 3: Now act out the roleplay in front of the class.

Info Point

A difficult topic: the salary.
The most important thing when negotiating the salary is to be well-informed. "What is a typical salary for this job in this region?", "How much does the company I applied to pay in general?" "What is my bottom-line?", etc.
In order to get an idea about salaries and cost of living in the region where you are looking for a job, consult the web pages listed on page 123. Further helpful links are www.homefair.com, www.wageweb.com and www.jobstar.org.

A job at the BBC

In the following job-description the Bristol Division of the BBC – Britain's largest broadcasting station – is looking for a production co-ordinator:

BBC

Working for equality of opportunity

Production Co-ordinator

Division: Bristol   Grade: 5   Reports to: Production Manager

The Production Co-ordinator provides logistical and co-ordination support to the production team on one or more productions, ensuring delivery on time and within budget.

BBC Bristol is looking to identify staff with the broad-range of skills necessary to work successfully as Production Coordinators across the Natural History Unit and Bristol Factual departments.

Bristol produces a wide range of output and recent titles include *Human Planet, Springwatch, Deadly 60, Nigel Slater's Simple Suppers, Cannabis: What's The Harm?, Paul Merton's Birth of Hollywood and Comic Relief documentaries and films for Comic Relief, Sport Relief and The One Show.*

Purpose
- To work in partnership with editorial colleagues to deliver outstanding, distinctive, multi-platform content by providing the ways to realise editorial ambitions within operational and financial constraints.
- To professionally co-ordinate production(s) using specialist production management skills, knowledge and experience.
- To drive continuous improvement throughout production.
- To contribute to and maintain a creative and collaborative culture.

Context
- Post holders at this level report to a Production Manager (or equivalent) and are responsible for the co-ordination of a production.
- They are expected to build and maintain a wide range of internal contacts from across the BBC.
- Typical external relationships will be with resource providers, artists and their agents, freelancers and public officials (e.g. local authorities).

Decision making authority

- Post holders at this level have delegated decision-making authority (from the Production Manager or equivalent) regarding the smooth day-to-day running of their production, working within BBC guidelines and frameworks.

Key outputs

Shape and plan productions

- Contributes to the scheduling and budgeting of the production in line with divisional requirements and relevant BBC frameworks, guidelines and policies.
- Responsible for supporting the Production Manager (or equivalent) in identifying and sourcing appropriate resource and location requirements for the production at the earliest possible stage.

Manage and deliver productions

- Responsible with editorial peers for ensuring compliance with BBC policies, guidelines, legislative and regulatory requirements, in order to minimise the BBC's exposure to risk. Escalates unresolved issues promptly.
- Responsible for ensuring all necessary rights are acquired and recorded for the complete delivery of the production, escalating any issues at the earliest stage.

Plan and manage production finances

- Responsible for preparing (or contributing to the preparation of), managing and monitoring production budgets, and for forecasting and reporting progress where required.
- Responsible for assessing the financial viability of content ideas that may arise during production, identifying any risks, and escalating issues if necessary.

Manage media assets

- Responsible for ensuring all deliverables are available in a timely manner to fulfil the commission and that post production "paperwork" is complete and accurate.

Manage the performance of production areas

- Identifies training needs of direct reports and ensures performance management arrangements are in place in line with BBC guidelines and policies.
- Supports diversity in every aspect of the production(s).

Skills, knowledge and experience

- Demonstrable experience of playing a co-ordinating role within a production team.
- Experience of delivering a range of/parts of productions on time and on budget and of co-ordinating deliverables for productions.
- Excellent organisational and planning skills – able to schedule and prioritise people and activities to meet operational deadlines.
- Able to use and advise on production systems and adopt new technologies on productions.
- Knows how to identify and source suitable resources and negotiate deals within given parameters.
- Demonstrable experience of working productively and collaboratively within a diverse production team.
- Experience of influencing and motivating others to achieve results.
- Essential business and finance skills – able to prepare, manage and/or monitor specific production resource plans and budgets.
- Well developed written and verbal communication skills.
- Knowledge of the BBC and the wider industry.

Competencies

Creative and Analytical Thinking Contributes creative ideas and helps translate them into practical plans.

Managing Relationships & Collaboration Able to build and maintain effective working relationships with a diverse range of people. Works collaboratively with others to solve problems. Shares ideas, knowledge and information across the BBC with colleagues.
Planning and Organising Co-ordinates many tasks simultaneously and maintains a high degree of accuracy and attention to detail. Organises and prioritises own and others' activities effectively in order to meet conflicting demands and deadlines.
Decision Making Able to evaluate the best course of action when faced with a problem or number of options. Knows when to refer to a more senior level. Uses initiative and takes responsibility for the consequences of own decisions.
Resilience Sustains performance and remains calm and in control when under pressure or in difficult situations. Is self-motivated and enthusiastic and works with the minimum of guidance and supervision.
Understanding Diversity – understands and appreciates the uniqueness of self and others. Demonstrates, and is committed to improving and understanding diversity. Able to articulate how individual differences can benefit the BBC.

To apply, please complete the 'Main Details' and 'Equal Opportunities' sections and upload a CV to the 'Additional Information Upload' section. In addition, in the 'Application Questions' section please provide details of your current salary and package and outline your interest in the role.

Quelle: BBC, Job Advert, https://careers.bbc.co.uk/fe/tpl_bbc01.asp?newms=jj&id=34426, [3.11.2011]

Words, words, words

to ensure – sicherstellen
constraint – Einschränkung
to contribute – beitragen
to source – beschaffen, beziehen
peer – Gleichgesinnter, Kollege
compliance – Einhaltung, Übereinstimmung
to escalate – eskalieren, ausweiten
viability – Durchführbarkeit
to prioritise – Prioritäten setzen
resilience – Ausdauer

Task 1

Look at the job advertisement and the BBC Homepage (www.bbc.co.uk). Answer these questions for yourself: What do you find interesting about this job and this company? What is not interesting? Which of the two posts would you rather apply for?
The chart below should help you to answer these questions:

Job-requirements	Personal qualities
Job 1	

Task 2

Write a **CV** using your own personal data. Remember to make a selection of your qualifications/interests that might be useful for the job.

Task 3

Write a **cover letter** following the scheme on pages 129–131.

Task 4

Now get together with a classmate who chose the same job as you did and roleplay a **job interview** between the applicant and the BBC recruiter. Switch roles.

A job at Peachpit's

By means of the job-description below, Peachpit Ltd – a publisher of educational books based in the US – is looking for a marketing coordinator:

Marketing Coordinator
The Marketing Coordinator is responsible for supporting the product marketing team for approximately 200 book titles annually. This includes coordinating a variety of marketing promotions, following processes for tracking information, knowing and using the Pearson systems that support product information and ensuring that all deadlines established by the sales organization for product information are met. The position requires excellent communication skills and the Coordinator will need to interact with key editorial and marketing staff as well as other Pearson departments. A high degree of attention to detail, strong computer skills and strong interpersonal skills are critical success factors for this position.

Qualifications

- Exemplary communication and interpersonal skills
- Superior organizational skills; ability to work independently and take initiative in prioritizing multiple deadlines
- Detail oriented and comfortable using Excel or other tracking software to manage deadlines and data
- A high level of computer proficiency, including but not limited to, the Microsoft Office software (Word, Excel, PowerPoint, File Maker Project); proven ability to quickly learn new systems
- B.A. in Marketing, Business, Journalism, preferred but will accept equivalent years of work experience
- Excellent problem solving skills
- Excellent written and verbal communication skills
- Proof reading and editing skills

- Demonstrated ability to juggle multiple tasks and balance a variety of priorities at the same time
- Ability to work well with internal departments, authors and a broad range of outside vendors to coordinate projects from start to finish

Responsibilities
- Serve as the centralized position for managing data that feeds the PTG sales process (NBIs and catalogs). Responsible for working with marketing managers to meet all sales deadlines for the national accounts and independent channel of titles/publications. This includes establishing tracking documents to manage the title lists, entering data into the HEPM, sending Peachpit descriptive copy and catalog copy to those within PTG who handle the information, reviewing catalog proofs and ensuring a high level of accuracy and quality for all title information. More specifically, the position will include: (60%)
- Coordination of the catalog data entry: coordinate catalog listing and publishing of titles in catalog; convert catalog copy to format required for each catalog and submit; ensure titles input have covers and are correctly added; proofread and update
- NBI/HEPM systems: convert copy from NBIs to enable information to be posted in the HEPM to feed out to online vendors, including web/online copy, catalog copy and author bios. Check all bibliographical information against titles and make changes
- Enter book product models from titles
- Pull the bestseller lists for retail catalog
- Enter targets into Greystoke
- Coordinate read-only for B&N, SNP and BXGY for Amazon
- Make corrections on Amazon.com and other online resellers
- Work with marketing team on the coordination of a variety of projects which can include developing and sending out author flyers, assisting in the creation of a Peachpit catalog, assistance in executing campaigns, assisting with user group mailings, and other marketing related activities
- Assist PMM in pulling bestseller lists and other marketing data
- Log reviews
- Work with Designer and with print vendors
- Work with Designer to create semi-annual catalog

About Peachpit
A Berkeley-based imprint of Pearson Education, Peachpit is a leading publisher of trade books for the computer graphics novice through professional. We offer a team-based atmosphere and a commitment to learning and growth for every employee; we encourage diversity in our organization.

Visit us at www.peachpit.com and www.pearsoned.com.

To apply for this position, please send a cover letter and resume to resumes@ peachpit.com with the job title "Marketing Coordinator" in the subject line. Include your resume in the body of the email or attach it as a Word document. Or write to:

Sheila Sugrue
Peachpit
1249 Eighth Street
Berkeley, CA 94710
EOE/M/F/D/V

Task

1. Look at the job advertisements and answer these questions for yourself: What do you find interesting about this job and this company? What is not interesting? The chart below should help you to answer these questions:

Job-requirements	Personal qualities

2. Write a **CV** using your own personal data. Remember to make a selection of your qualifications/interests that might be useful for the job.
3. Write a **cover letter** following the scheme on pages 129–131.
4. Now get together with a classmate who chose the same job as you did and role-play a **job interview** between the applicant and Peachpit's recruiter. Switch roles.

A job in marketing

Maddox Marketing Group, Inc

Marketing Assistant

Product/Services:
Advertising Agency – Marketing Communications and Creative Services

Duties/Responsibilities:
This entry level position is responsible for supporting the agency by greeting office visitors, answering phones, facilitating project management process, typing/preparing proposals and presentations, office administration, prospect research, database management, appointment setting, project coordination, networking and public relations support. The person in this position will act as a liaison between prospects, clients, account director(s) and creative studio of the agency assuring effective communication and client project execution.

Qualifications:
Successful candidate will have at least one year of office administrative or sales support experience in an advertising agency, corporate marketing/sales department or professional services environment. Must have strong organization, writing and communication skills. Must also have a good working knowledge of Mac OSX and be proficient in office communication, CRM and presentation software. Web and interactive media content development and maintenance experience a plus.

Advancement:
This is an entry level support position. Advancement will be contingent on performance. Over time, candidate will take on more solo responsibility for coordinating projects and managing client relationships. The person in this position is expected to grow into an account manager position. Agency also provides for seminar and other continued learning opportunities.

Compensation/Benefits:
This is a fulltime, salaried, entry level position. Starting salary negotiable depending on experience. Compensation package also includes eligibility for participation in the company health insurance, vacation and bonus plans.

How to apply:
Please email, mail or fax your resume with salary history and requirements to:

Rob Maddox - SR
Maddox Marketing Group, Inc
2291 Riverfront Parkway, Suite 200
Cuyahoga Falls, OH 44221

E-Mail: mmghr@maddoxmarketing.com

Phone: 330-945-6232
Fax: 330-945-6290

Words, words, words

advancement – Beförderung
contingent on – abhängig von
CRM – Customer Relationship Management
eligibility – Berechtigung
entry level position – Einstiegsposition
liaison – Zusammenarbeit
to be proficient in – gut sein in
prospect – hier: potenzieller Kunde

Task

1. Answer these questions for yourself: What do you find interesting about this job and this company? What is not interesting? Do you fulfil the requirements for this job? The chart below should help you to answer these questions:

Job-requirements	Personal qualities

2. Write a **CV** using your own personal data. Remember to make a selection of your qualifications/interests that might be useful for the job.

3. Write a **cover letter** following the scheme on pages 129–131.
4. Now get together with a classmate and roleplay a **job interview** between the applicant and the Maddox recruiter. Switch roles.

A job as event manager in London

Task 1

Decide on one of the jobs on the following pages.

Get together with a classmate who has picked the same job.

Imagine you are a potential applicant: What kind of information would you ask your potential employer in a first phone call. Imagine you are the contact mentioned in the ad: What kind of information would you need to give a potential applicant who calls.

Role-play the phone call in front of the class.

Info Point

Refresh your knowledge about telephoning by returning to unit 3 on page 45 and the corresponding skill file (page 148) to be able to perform a professional call with an appropriate beginning and close.

Task 2

On the basis of the ad and the information you have received, write a cover letter for the advertised job.

Complete the application by writing a CV which is especially suitable for the job you picked.

Task 3

You have been invited for a job interview. Role-play the interview together with a classmate who has picked the same ad in front of the class.

Chemistry seeks Events Manager
Chemistry, the UK's largest live dating experience, is looking for a bright enthusiastic Events Manager with a minimum of 1-2 years events planning experience, with a proven track record.

Duties will include:
- identifying appropriate venues for events through research and site visits
- negotiating the provision of space and services with venues
- ensuring contracts are signed for all venues
- working together with venue managers up to and post event
- ensuring all events are commercially viable and maintaining accurate financial records for each event
- organising suppliers for event consumables and PR materials
- exploring of new venues and types of events within the company's aims
- identifying and exploring new cities for the brand
- additional duties as required

The ideal candidate will be an organised planner who has commitment and passion and much determination. This is an excellent opportunity to join this vibrant company, you will need to be able to plan and execute "Singles Events" throughout the UK and to budget and oversee all aspects of each event. These "Singles Events" will range in size from as little as 100 guests to over 2000 guests per event.

This position will require travel across the UK with overnight stays, therefore, the ideal candidate must have a flexible approach and be willing to travel.

Additional Information
Salary: to GBP 20,000.00 per year
Position Type: Full Time, Permanent

Contact Information
Sarah Whatshername
Sarah.whatshername@t-offlinechemistry.com

www.chemistry.co.uk

Marketing Communications Event Co-ordinator, West London
We are currently seeking an experienced Marketing Communications Event Co-ordinator to support the planning and execution of large and complex EMEA and global corporate events, for our blue chip technology client. If you are a true self-starter and enjoy being part of a focused, results-driven marketing communications team, and you have previous experience in event co-ordination in the technology or telecommunications sectors, please contact us now.

The Role
£27,000 – £30,000 per annum pro rata depending on experience
22 days paid holiday per annum pro rata
Initial contract to the end of this year with possibility of extension subject to performance and client strategic planning. Monthly travel across EMEA and bi-annual travel to the US. To work for, and be on the payroll of, Wilson Miller Resourcing but based within the event team of one of our key blue chip technology clients based in West London.

The Marketing Communication Event Co-ordinator will support one of the programme managers in the planning and delivery of a premier annual technical event, as part of an EMEA focused event marketing team. The programme comprises four regional events which take place in September, October and December. You are to support the Programme Manager in developing and maintaining the project plan, event objectives and strategy, in relation to the management of the finance strategy, maintenance of the budget, and event timelines and is to manage existing or source new third party agencies. The position implies working cross functionally across global, channel, corporate marketing, technical marketing, partner organisations, web and event teams to ensure the successful delivery of the event programme. The Co-ordinator is to support the Programme Manager in defining and organising the attendance, internal and external communications, content, production,
PR, sponsorship and measurement programmes. Besides you are responsible for the execution of the measurement and post event analysis programme. The successful candidate should also be able to promote conference events to potential sponsors both internally and externally, create databases and liaise with data service providers. You should be able to establish and manage relationships with the marketing community and has to attend Event Marketing Team meetings every six weeks and the weekly conference call. Responsibility includes overall conference and project management, post conference results analysis, measurement and outcome reporting. The candidate is expected to work in a self sufficient manner with minimal supervision.

The Person
Will have 1 + years' experience in worldwide or EMEA business to business event co-ordination. The majority of this experience should be in the technology or telecommunications sectors. You should have proven expertise in conference event marketing support, project management, co-ordination, budget management and post event analysis. You should be able to manage external agencies. We expect first class problem solving skills, a proven lateral and creative thinker with high level of attention to detail. The person should be persuasive, confident and charismatic with the ability to build relationships in a fast-paced changing environment. Intelligent, articulate, flexible, committed and able to work collaboratively. We are looking for a self-motivated and proactive person who is prepared to take the initiative and commited to 'add value' and 'over deliver' to guarantee success. This self-sufficient, resourceful and responsive person should ideally have excellent personal, verbal and written presentation skills in English (presentation at senior level will be required). The ability to speak intermediate French would be a distinct advantage. We also expect competence in Microsoft office suite, excel, PowerPoint and an excellent computer literacy. Likely to be a high calibre graduate and/or have a marketing qualification (CIM or similar).

How to apply
Please send your CV plus details of your current salary package and notice period to: Chris Huge at candidates@wilsonmiller.co.uk. First interviews will take place in Chelmsford. Further assessments will be made by our client at their West London office. Only shortlisted candidates will be contacted. Candidates must be eligible to work in the UK before submitting their CV. Agencies should not apply.

Additional Information
Position Type: Full Time
Ref Code: 191KL

Contact Information
Chris Huge
Wilson Miller Resourcing Ltd

Skill files

Giving presentations and writing reports

Before you prepare a presentation or a report, the most important thing to ask yourself is your objective. With a presentation you usually have the choice between either informing your audience about something or convincing it. With a report your objective will be to inform, to explain, to analyse, to justify or to recommend. In order to support this objective it is helpful to consider the following questions:

1. Who is your audience/are your readers?
2. What is the best format?
3. What is the best structure?
4. What style should you use?
5. How should you give recommendations?

Concerning your audience/readers you should ask yourself whether the audience is internal or external, what their position in the company hierarchy is and what their expectations are concerning content and format.

Presentation

Signposting

Similar to signs in the street showing you the way, you also have to guide your audience through your presentation. This can easily be done by putting out language signals throughout your presentation indicating its structure.

Function	**Language**
Ordering	• Firstly, …, secondly, …, thirdly, …, lastly … • First of all, …, then, …, next, …, after that, …, finally, … • To start with, …, later, …, to finish up, ….
Introducing your subject	• I would like to start by outlining … • First of all, I will introduce … • Starting with …
Finishing one subject	• That's all I have to say about … • We have looked at … • So much for …
Starting a new subject	• Let me now turn to … • Now we will move on to … • Next …
Analysing a point and giving recom-mendations	• Let us consider this in more detail … • What does this mean for ABC? • Where does that lead us?
Giving an example	• For example … • A good example of this is … • To illustrate this point …
Dealing with questions	• I will come back to this question later in my talk … • Perhaps you would like to raise this point later at the end … • I would like to deal with this question later if I may …
Summarising	• Let us summarise briefly what we have looked at … • If I can just sum up the main points … • Finally let me remind you of some of the issues we have covered …

Vocabulary for visualisation

Presenting is not just about talking but also about visualising what you are talking about. In order to be able to refer to this, the following vocabulary can be used:

Visualisation media		**Charts, graphs and tables**	
electronic media		charts	Diagramm
beamer	Beamer	bar chart	Balkendiagramm
screen	Bildschirm, Leinwand	pie chart	Kreis-/Kuchendiagramm
overhead projector (OHP)	Overheadprojektor	flow chart	Flussdiagramm
(overhead) transparency	Folie		

slide projector	Diaprojektor	(line)graph	Kurve(ndiagramm)
slide	Dia, PowerPoint Folie		
pointer	(Laser)pointer	diagram	Diagramm
classic media		table	Tabelle
blackboard	Tafel	spreadsheet	(Excel-)tabelle
whiteboard	Kunststofftafel		
flip chart	Flipchart		
chalk	Kreide		

Writing reports

Vocabulary for linking language

The way messages in a report are linked together has a strong influence on the transparency of the text. This can be achieved by using specific expressions which help to link together sentences and paragraphs.

Linking concept	**Language**
generalising	usually, typically, normally
giving examples	for example, for instance, such as, as follows
highlighting	especially, in particular, indeed
adding	in addition, furthermore, moreover
consequences	therefore, so, consequently
reasons	because, in order to
introducing effects	this led to, this resulted in, this caused

Small talk

Small talk has nothing to do with size. It is meant to be light social conversation. That way people show interest in their conversation partners and establish a friendly atmosphere. At a social event such as a party most of the conversation is small talk. At a business meeting, on the phone or at an interview, conversation usually starts and ends with a few minutes of small talk. It can also take place as a short break from business talk during meetings or telephone calls. On these occasions, facts and figures, definitive statements and direct confrontation should be avoided. In order to keep a conversation going, it is helpful to ask open questions which require the conversation partner to reply with more than yes or no. The same goes for answering questions. Also, adding extra information keeps a conversation going.

Topics for small talk

+	–
the weather	age
a journey (to or from the place where you are)	income
being in GB/US for the first time	religion
things to do and see in the area	illness
cultural events	politics
sports, films, books	criticising country
anything that is not controversial	anything controversial
anything that is not too personal	anything personal

Small talk with unknown business visitors for the first time

Responding
Really? I didn't know that.
Oh, that's interesting.
That's right.
I couldn't agree more.

Starting a conversation
Hello.
How are things?
Is this your first visit to Germany?
How was your trip/journey/flight?
Did you have any difficulties finding us?
Lovely weather today, isn't it?
Have you been away yet this year?

Finishing a conversation
It was nice talking to you.
Excuse me, I've got to go now.
Enjoy the rest of your time/stay in Germany.
Hope to see you again soon.
Goodbye.

Small talk between acquaintances

If you are talking to colleagues whom you know already but have not seen for a while, you can relate to topics you have in common or that relate to your conversation partner:

- How are things going, Mr Miller?
- Have you finished preparing for the party yet, Ms Jones?
- What do you think our bonus will be like this month?

From small talk to business

If you do not know the rules, you can stick to small talk for hours. Therefore it is helpful to have some expressions in order to move on to business.

- Anyway, the reason I wanted to meet you is to discuss the layout of our new marketing brochure.
- Ok, we should probably get down to business now.

Telephoning

The international telephone alphabet

When spelling or noting names over the phone one ought to use the official international telephone alphabet in order to be understood by anyone in the world. Originally, this alphabet, developed by NATO, was used by military and radio operators.

Letter	Pronunciation	International telephone alphabet
A	[eɪ]	ALPHA
B	[bi:]	BRAVO
C	[si:]	CHARLIE
D	[di:]	DELTA
E	[i:]	ECHO
F	[ef]	FOXTROT
G	[dʒi:]	GOLF
H	[eItʃ]	HOTEL
I	[aI]	INDIA
J	[dʒeI]	JULIET
K	[keɪ]	KILO
L	[el]	LIMA
M	[em]	MIKE
N	[en]	NOVEMBER
O	[əU]	OSCAR
P	[pi:]	PAPA
Q	[kju:]	QUEBEC
R	[a:]	ROMEO
S	[es]	SIERRA
T	[ti:]	TANGO
U	[ju:]	UNIFORM
V	[vi:]	VICTOR
W	[dʌblju:]	WHISKY
X	[eks]	X-RAY
Y	[waɪ]	YANKEE
Z	[zed]	ZULU

"Capital Romeo" means "R" as opposed to "r". If you have to spell a German letter with an umlaut ("ä", "ö", "ü"), say "Alpha umlaut" or "Alpha Echo" and so on.

In order to make learning the sounds of the letters easier, group them together according to the same sound:

[eɪ]	[i:]	[e]	[aɪ]	[əʊ]	[ju:]	[a:]
A	B	F	I	O	Q	R
H	C	L	Y		U	
J	D	M			W	
K	E	N				
	G	S				
	P	X				
	T	Z				
	V					

Telephone Etiquette

Apart from the international telephone alphabet, English speakers also often use other common words. If you do so please remember to say "D as in day" or "D for dog" rather than "D dog".

Time zones

Especially when doing business with companies based overseas, it is important to keep in mind the different time zones. You can use the following chart in order to calculate what the best time is for telephoning somebody in the US for instance.

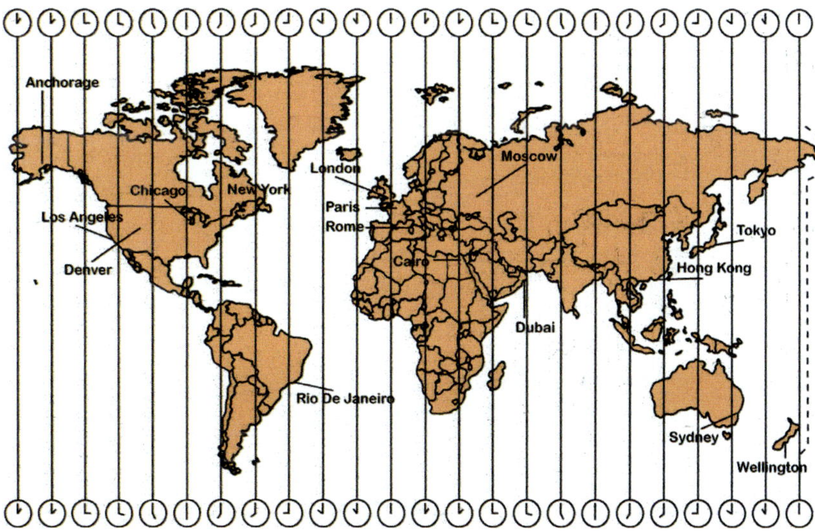

The time

There can be confusion when mentioning the time: "10:30 am" is often referred to as "half ten" instead of "half past ten".
Obviously, this has nothing to do with the German "halb zehn", which is 9:30. Of course this also goes for 8:30, 9:30, 11:30 etc.

Numbers

Spelling numbers
When you dictate or note down a telephone number read it back to your telephone partner in order to check whether it is written down correctly.

- Read each number separately: "123642" is read "1-2-3-6-4-2" rather than "twelve, thirty-six, fourty-two".
- When a number occurs twice such as "33", it is read as "double three" rather than "thirty-three".
- "0" is spelled as the letter "o" or "zero": "7439660" is spelled as "seven-four-three-nine-double-six-oh/zero".

• 215	two hundred and fifteen
• 7,234	seven thousand, two hundred and thirty-four
• 6,856,252	six million, eight hundred fifty-six, two-hundred fifty-two
• 4.1536	four point one five three six*

• EUR36.27	thirty-six euros, (and) twenty-seven (cents)
• $12.52	twelve dollars, (and) fifty-two (cents)

* In English a comma shows thousands, and a point shows the decimal place.

Dates

The date can be said in different ways depending on the way it is written or the country where it is used.
March 31, 2012 can be said as
"the thirty-first of March, two thousand and twelve"
"March thirty-first, two thousand and twelve" (American English)

The date 03.02.12 means February 3, 2012 in Great Britain, but 2 March in the USA.

Symbols

Symbol	Pronounciation
.	point (numbers), full stop/period (at the end of a sentence), dot (in e-mail or website address)
,	comma
:	colon
;	semi-colon
?	question mark
!	exclamation mark
x_x	underscore
X-X	hyphen
X–X	dash
@	at
/	(forward) slash
\	back slash
#	hash/pound/number (sign)
*	asterisk/star
(	open bracket
)	close bracket
( )	round brackets
[ ]	square brackets

Active listening strategies

In order to indicate to your telephone conversation partner that you continue to listen and to show interest, agreement and understanding, there are different strategies such as

Backchannelling
Listen in a "noisy" way by commenting.

Oh, I see ...
Mmmm
Oh, that sounds interesting.
Well ...
OK ...
That sounds like a real problem!
That's one good thing at least.
OK, I've got that.
Of course.

Echoing
Repeat what you have heard.

A: We meet again on Monday.
B: Monday. Right.

Reading back
Repeat something to get a confirmation.

A: My email is cmueller@t-online.de.
B: Let me just read that back to you. So that's cmueller@t-online.de.

Clarifying
Make sure that you understood something correctly.

A: Our office is at 30 York Street.
B: Sorry, was that 30 or 13?

Video-conferencing

In times of cost-effective managing telephone- and video-conferencing has become even more popular than before in order to avoid too much travelling and associated costs. This is especially true for companies with an American business culture who often have regular conferences in Germany as part of their reporting structure. These telephone- and/or video-conferences also include the ability to transmit a powerpoint presentation at the same time, which is usually discussed and referred to afterwards. Usually, there is a chairperson who also takes care of the order of the participants' contributions. The participants inform the chairperson via instant messaging about their wish to contribute and are given a talking slot by the chairperson. Therefore it takes a lot of discipline to behave according to the situation in order to contribute adequately.

Translating

When translating a text from English into German, the following procedure might be helpful for you.

Info Point

First step

Read the whole text carefully and make notes in German.

Second step

Write a first version in pencil so that you can rework it easily later on. Keep to the surface structure of the text as closely as possible, but do not translate word for word.

Third step

Re-read your first version eliminating any gaps you have left in your translation. Use a dictionary if necessary.

Fourth step

Re-read your improved text again and see if it sounds German. If not, try to think about what you intend to say in German and make corrections. If necessary, repeat these steps.

False friends

In the following list you will find words which can be confusing for German speaking people. In the first column you find the German expression you intend to say. The second column gives you the correct English word. The 'false friend' is in the column headed "You should NOT say", followed by the German equivalent.

There are, of course, 'true friends'. You will find a list below.

You mean	You should say	You should NOT say	Why not?
absolvieren	complete	absolve	= lossprechen, freisprechen
adäquat	appropriate/suitable	adequate	= ausreichend, genügend
aktuell	current, recent, up to date	actual	= tatsächlich, eigentlich
also	so, it seems	also	= auch
Band	volume	band	= Musikgruppe, das Band
bekommen	have, get	become	= werden
Branche	field, industry, line of business	branch	= Zweigstelle, Filiale

You mean	You should say	You should NOT say	Why not?
Chef	boss	chef, chief	= Chefkoch, Häuptling
dezent	subtle, discreet	decent	= anständig
Direktion	management	direction	= Richtung, Anweisung
engagiert	hard-working	engaged	= verlobt, besetzt (Tel.)
familiär	personal	familiar	= (wohl)bekannt
forcieren	push, force on	force	= zwingen
Fusion	merger	fusion	= Verschmelzung (techn.)
genial	brilliant, ingenious	genial	= herzlich, zuvorkommend
Grad	degree	grade	= (Güte)klasse, Schulnote
Gymnasium	secondary/grammar/high school	gymnasium	= Turnhalle, Sportstudio
handeln (mit)	deal (in), trade	handle	= handhaben, bearbeiten
Handy	mobile/cell(ular) phone	handy	= praktisch, handlich
Hochschule	university, college	high school	= Sekundarschule (AE)
irritieren	confuse	irritated	= genervt, verärgert
jobben	work (as a temp)	(to) job	("job" ist kein Verb im Engl.!)
Kaution	(safety) deposit	caution	= Vorsicht, Warnung
Konfession	religion, religious denomination	confession	= Geständnis, Beichte
Lektüre	reading (matter)	lecture	= Vorlesung, Vortrag
Mappe	folder, file	map	= (Land)karte
meinen	think, feel	mean	= bedeuten, sagen wollen
Notiz	note	notice	= Benachrichtigung
offensiv	vigorous, aggressive	offensive	= beleidigend
pathetisch	emotional, empassioned	pathetic	= armselig
Preis (bei Wettbewerben)	prize, award	price	= Preis (für eine Ware)
per (z. B. per Bahn)	by, via	per	= pro (z. B. in pro Person)
prinzipiell	in principle	principally	= in erster Linie
Prospekt	brochure, leaflet	prospect	= Aussicht, Chance
Protokoll	minutes, report	protocol	= Vorgehensweise (dipl.)
Provision	commission	provision	= Vorkehrung
Prozess (Gericht)	trial, lawsuit	process	= Prozess, Ablauf

Skill files

You mean	You should say	You should NOT say	Why not?
rationell	efficient	rational	= logisch, rational
Sender (TV)	(TV, radio) station	sender	= Absender
sensibel	sensitive	sensible	= vernünftig
Smoking	dinner jacket, tuxedo (US)	smoking	= Rauchen
sparen	save	spare	= verschonen, befreien von
Stadium	stage, level	stadium	= vernünftig
sympathisch	nice, likeable	sympathetic	= mitfühlend, einfühlsam
synchronisiert	dubbed	synchro-nized	= zeitlich abgestimmt
überhören	not hear	overhear	= zufällig hören
Unternehmer/in	businessman/wom-an, entrepreneur	undertaker	= Leichenbestatter
virtuos	brilliant, highly skilled	virtuous	= tugendhaft

True friends

Words which are more or less identical

German	English
Alphabet	alphabet
Altar	altar
Anorak	anorak
Arm	arm
Ball	ball
Ballett	ballet
Band	band
Bank (Gebäude)	bank
Basketball	basketball
bitter	bitter
blind	blind
blond	blond
Boss	boss
bringen	bring
Bus	bus

German	English
Butter	butter
Chance	chance
Code	code
Computer	computer
Cousin	cousin
Dessert	dessert
Drama	drama
Experiment	experiment
extra	extra
fair	fair
Film	film
finden	find
Finger	finger
Firma	firm
fit	fit

German	English
Frost	frost
Funktion	function
Gas	gas
Gold	gold
Golf	golf
Hammer	hammer
Hand	hand
Hotel	hotel
Hunger	hunger
Ideal	ideal
Illusion	illusion
Instrument	instrument
Jeans	jeans
Kindergarten	kindergarten (pre-school (AE))
Kitsch	kitsch
Material	material
minus	minus
modern	modern
Moment	moment
Museum	museum
Name	name
Nation	nation
Orange	orange
packen	pack
Partner	partner
Person	person
Pilot	pilot
plus	plus
Pony	pony
Post	post

German	English
Pudding	pudding
Pullover	pullover
Radio	radio
Rest	rest
Ring	ring
Rose	rose
Rucksack	rucksack
Ski	ski
Sofa	sofa
Spray	spray
Stress	stress
Talent	talent
Taxi	taxi
Team	team
Test	test
Text	text
Tiger	tiger
Toast	toast
Toilette	toilet
Trainer	trainer
Uniform	uniform
Vase	vase
Video	video
Volleyball	volleyball
Waldsterben	waldsterben
warm	warm
Wind	wind
Winter	winter
Wolf	wolf
Zebra	zebra

Words which are nearly identical

German	English
Akzent	accent
Alkohol	alcohol
Artikel	article
Assistent	assistant
automatisch	automatic
Banane	banana
Bett	bed
beginnen	to begin
Bibel	bible
Bier	beer
Biologie	Biology
Bluse	blouse
Bombe	bomb
braun	brown
Büfett	buffet
Bulle	bull
Busch	bush
Elefant	elephant
Experte	expert
fallen	fall
Figur (Körper)	figure
Fisch	fish
Funktion	function
Garten	garden
Geografie	Geography
Glas	glass
Gras	grass
grillen	grill
Gymnastik	gymnastics
Henne	hen
Horoskop	horoscope
Hut	hat
Insekt	insect
Kaffee	coffee
Kalender	calendar

German	English
Kandidat	candidate
Karotte	carrot
Karte (allgemein)	card
Karton	carton
Kassette	cassette
Kathedrale	cathedral
Klasse	class
Komplex	complex
Kontinent	continent
Kontrolle	control
Konzept	concept
Konzert	concert
Korridor	corridor
Kostüm	costume
kulturell	cultural
Kurs	course
Keller	cellar
Klub	club
Lippe	lip
Manuskript	manuscript
Markt	market
Marsch	march
Mathematik	mathematics
Medizin	medicine
Metall	metal
Meter	metre
Methode	method
Milch	milk
Musik	music
Nerven	nerves
Öl	oil
Oper	opera
Ozean	ocean
Partei	party
Patient	patient

German	English
Physik	physics
Politik	politics
Präsident	president
radikal	radical
Ratte	rat
Respekt	respect
Rezeption	reception
Salz	salt
Sänger	singer
Schmuggler	smuggler
Schock	shock
Sekunde	second
Silber	silver
Socken	socks
Sommer	summer

German	English
Sport	sport (not school subject)
Stil	style
Sturm	storm
Strategie	strategy
systematisch	systematically
Taktik	tactics
Temperatur	temperature
Titel	title
Tomate	tomato
Traktor	tractor
Unterwelt	underworld
Wurm	worm
Zentrum	centre, center (AE)

How to write a treatment

(Special skill file for the audiovisual media business)

What exactly is a treatment? A treatment is a marketing tool; a document used to sell a producer your story and purchase the rights to it. Secondly, it helps the writer organise their own thoughts. It saves time if you know what you're writing about and it makes it easier to discuss your work with an editor.

A treatment is **not** a synopsis. It is not a summary of your script. A treatment is a compelling narrative of a story intended for production as a feature film or a TV movie. The length of a treatment can vary from five to fifty pages depending on the purpose.

Treatments are ALWAYS written in **simple language prose** and in the **present tense**. They are the broad strokes of the story and tell about the setting of the story, the characters in the story, the turning points of the story and the most dramatic scenes in the story.

If you choose to include any dramatic pieces of **dialogue**, write them **in prose**, i.e. "he tells her that he's leaving" or keep the dialogue to a minimum and place in quotes … "It's over." Be sure to place **character names in capitals** when first introduced.

When writing a treatment, think visual. **Paint a picture** of the scenes. For example something like this: "It's hot. Not just hot. Killer hot. Steam rises from the street. Huge, black clouds roll into the city that refuses to die. Palm trees bend almost in half. Suddenly, the skies open up above NASA headquarters."

Use words that **appeal to the senses** when writing treatments. Although the primary sense that you'll want to use is visual, don't forget auditory and sensual (touch) words, e. g. "The WHIRR of the helicopter blades …"

Don't drown your readers with details about the story. You'll bore them to death and you won't make a sale. Know what the theme or point of your story is and sell it.

Here are the components of a good treatment:

1. **Introduction:** Start with an opening that hooks the reader. The introduction should be written in the style of a jacket copy, i. e. not necessarily in a logical sequence, but picking on the most salient aspects. It should be between 5 and 20 lines and must make great claims for the work. A useful approach to writing the introduction is simply to state the setting, then describe the key dramatic incident(s), leaving the reader desperate to know what happens next!
2. **Character biographies:** Introduce the reader to your protagonist and other important characters. For major characters, write between 5 and 10 lines, for minor characters 3 to 5 lines is usually enough. It is essential to make clear who the main character is and what motivates them. Try to give the reader some psychological and personal insights into your characters, describe in an impressionistic way what they look like (e. g. tall or short, not 6 foot 2 inches) and what their attitudes to life are.
3. **Treatment:** Show what the main conflict of the story is and what type of story it is (drama, suspense, action, comedy, etc.). Explain the story line (spine) and structure of the story. This section should include the major scenes of the movie and the turning points (act breaks). The style should be like a scene-by-scene summary and should reflect the pace of the movie. End with a knockout ending that makes the reader want to shout "YES!".

Vocabulary

VOCABULARY

German – English

A

A&R Manager (Musikbusiness)	A&R representative (n)
abfallen	drop (v)
abfallen	fall (v)
ableiten von	derive from (v)
abnehmen	decrease (v), go down (v), decline (v)
Abonnement	subscription (n)
Abonnement-Service	subcription service (n)
abrutschen	slump (v)
Abschluss (Schule, Uni)	degree (n)
abschweifen	digress (v)
absichern	ensure (v)
Abstimmung, eine – vornehmen	take a vote (v)
Abstimmung, geheime	secret ballot (n)

Abstimmung, sich einer – enthalten	abstain from a vote (v)
Abteilung	department (n)
Abteilungsleiter	head of department (n)
Ähnlichkeit	similarity (n)
akquirieren	acquire (v)
Akquise	acquisition (n)
am Apparat	speaking
am Apparat bleiben	stay on the line (v)
anbinden	commit (v)
Änderung	amendment (n)
anfordern	request (v)
anfragen	request (v)
angemessen	appropriate (adj)
Angestellter	employee (n)
Angestellte	employee (n)
Anhang, Datei –	attachment (n)
anhängen (Datei)	attach (v)
Anlage	attachment (n)
Anruf	call (n)
Anruf, abgehender	outgoing call (adj)
Anruf, einen – entgegennehmen	take/answer a call (v)
Anruf, eingehender	incoming call (adj)
Anrufbeantworter	answering machine, voice-mail, answer- phone (n)
Anrufe, keine – durchstellen	hold all calls (v)
anrufen	call/make a call (v)
anrufen, jemanden –	call somebody (v), ring somebody (v)
anschaffen	acquire (v)
Anschaffung	acquisition (n)
Anschreiben bei einer Bewerbung	cover letter (n)
ansteigen	increase (v), rise (v), grow (v), go up (v)
anstellen	employ (v)
Anteilsnehmer	stakeholder (n)

Antrag	motion (n)
Antrag, einen – ablehnen	defeat a motion (v), reject a motion (v)
Antrag, einen – annehmen	pass/carry a motion (v)
Antrag, einen – fallen lassen	drop a motion (v)
Antrag, einen – stellen	propose a motion (v)
Antrag, einen – unterstützen	second a motion (v)
Antrag, einen – zurückstellen	shelve a motion (v)
Anwenderfreundlichkeit	userfriendliness (n)
Anwendung	application (n)
Anwendung, Einsatz	deployment (n)
Anwerber für Personal	recruiter (n)
Anzeichen	indication (n)
Anzeige, gestaltete –	display ad(vertisement) (n)
Anzeigenabteilung	advertising department (n)
anziehen	attract (v)
Apparat	device (n)
appellieren, ansprechen	appeal to (v)
Arbeitgeber	employer (n)
Arbeitsteilung	division of labour (n)
Art Director	art director (n)
Artwork (z. B. Zeichnungen, Fotos, die zu Werbezwecken verwendet werden)	artwork (n)
Assistent (Beleuchtung, Bühne)	best boy (n)
Attraktion	gimmick (n)
auf einem Niveau bleiben	stay at the same level (v)
aufbauen	establish (v)
aufeinanderfolgend	subsequent (adj)
Aufhänger	hook (n)
Auflage	circulation (n)
auflegen	hang up (v)
Auflösung	resolution (n)

Vocabulary

Aufmerksamkeit, die – von jdm. erlangen	grab someone's attention (v)
Aufnahme	shot (n)
Aufnahmeleiter	location manager (n)
Aufnahmezubehör	recording gear (n)
Auftrag, um einen – konkurrierende Agenturen	pitch (n)
Auftragsvergabe	print buying (n)
Aufzeichnungen	notes, records (n)
ausbauen	strengthen (v)
ausdrücken, klar –	articulate (v)
ausgeliefert sein	hit the shelf (v)
ausgeprägt	marked (adj)
Aushängeschild	flagship (n)
Ausland, im –	abroad (adj)
auslassen	omit (v)
ausreichen	suffice (v)
ausreichend	sufficient (adj)
ausrichten auf	gear to (v)
ausrichten, jemandem etwas –	give somebody a message (v)
Ausschreibung, eine – machen	call for tenders (v)
Ausschusssitzung	committee meeting (n)
äußerst	utmost (adj)
austauschbar	interchangeably (adv), interchangeable (adj)
Austragungsort	venue (n)
ausweiten	expand (v)
Auswirkung	impact (n)
Auszubildende/r	trainee (n)

B

Bandenwerbung	pitch-perimeter advertising (n)
bearbeiten	process (v)
bedienen	operate (v)

Bedrohung	threat (n)
Bedürfnis	need (n)
befördern	promote (v)
befördert werden	to be promoted
Befragung	interview (n), survey (n)
Begeisterung	enthusiasm (n)
begleiten	escort (v)
beifügen	attach (v)
Beilage	insert (n)
beitragen	contribute (v)
bekannt, etwas als – voraussetzen	take sth. as read (v)
bekömmlich	wholesome (adj)
Belegschaft	staff (n)
Beleuchtung	lighting (n)
Belletristik	genre fiction (n)
Bemühen	endeavor (n)
beraten	advise (v), consult (v)
Bereitschaft	commitment (n)
Berufstätiger	professional (n)
beschäftigen	employ (v)
Beschluss	resolution (n)
beschlussfähig sein	have a quorum (v)
Beschränkung	constraint (n)
beschützen	protect (v)
besetzt	busy (AE) (adj), engaged (BE) (adj)
Besetztzeichen	busy signal (n), engaged tone (AE: busy signal) (n)
Besprechung, an einer – teilnehmen	take part in a meeting (v)
Besprechung, ein – abhalten	hold/have a meeting (v)
Besprechung, eine – absagen	cancel a meeting (v)
Besprechung, eine – ansetzen	fix, schedule, set up a meeting (v)
Besprechung, eine – verschieben	postpone a meeting (v)

Besprechungstermin, einen – festlegen	arrange/fix a meeting (v)
bestätigen, etwas –	confirm something (v)
bestehen aus	consist of (v)
betonen	emphasise (v)
beträchtlich	substantial (adj)
Betreuer, z. B. von Kunden	account manager (n)
Betriebswirtschaftslehre	business studies (n)
Betroffener	stakeholder (n)
Beutezug	foray (n)
bewandert (i.S.v. sich mit etw. gut auskennen)	literate (adj)
Bewerber	applicant (n)
Bewerbung	job application (n), application (n)
Bewerbungsgespräch	job interview (n)
bewerten	evaluate (v), assess (v)
bewerten, sich selbst –	self-assess (v)
Beziehung	relationship (n)
Bildunterschrift	caption (n)
Bockkran	cherrypicker (n)
Branchenverzeichnis	yellow pages (n)
Briefing zu einer Werbekampagne	advertising brief (n)
Buchhalter	accountant (n)
Buchhaltungsabteilung	accounts department (n)
buchstabieren, etwas –	spell something (v)
Bühne	stage (n)
Bürokollege	officemate (n)
Büronummer	work number (n)

C

Caster	casting director (n)
Chance	opportunity (n)
Chef vom Dienst	sub editor (n)
Chefredakteur	editor (n)

D

dafür sein	be in favour of (v)
Denken, logisches	reasoning (n)
deutlich	sharp (adj), marked (adj), clear (adj)
Dia, Folie (bei *Powerpoint*-Präsentation)	slide (n)
Diplomarbeit	thesis (n)
Disziplinarmaßnahmen	disciplinary action (n)
Dolly	dolly (n)
Dreh	shooting (n)
Drehbuch	script (n)
Drehbuchauszüge	script breakdown (n)
Drehplan	shooting schedule (n)
dringend	urgent (adj)
Druckerzeugnis	print product (n)
Durchschlag	carbon copy (n)
durchstellen, jemanden (zu jemandem) –	put somebody through (to somebody) (v)
durchstöbern	roam through (v)
Durchwahl	direct line (n), extension (n)

E

Effekt	impact (n)
Einfühlungsvermögen	empathy (n)
einführen	launch (v)
Einführung (Markt)	launch (n)
Einheit	unit/charge (n)
Einigung, eine – erzielen	reach a consensus (v)
einkaufen	purchase (v)
Einkäufer von Medialeistungen	media buyer (n)
Einkommen	revenue (n)
einpendeln, sich	flatten out (v), level off (v)
einschätzen	assess (v)
Einschränkung	constraint (n)
einstellen	adjust (v)

Einstellungsstopp	freeze on recruitment (n)
einstimmig	unanimous (adj)
Einwand, einem – stattgeben	accept an objection (v)
Einwand, einen – zurückweisen	overrule an objection (v)
Einwände erheben	raise objections (v)
Einzelhandel	retail (n)
Einzelhandelsgeschäft	retail outlet (n)
Einzelhändler	retailer (n)
einzigartig	unique (adj)
empfehlenswert	recommendable (adj)
Empfehlung	recommendation (n)
Engagement	commitment (n)
Enthaltung	abstention (n)
enthüllen	unveil (v)
Entlassung	dismissal (n)
erforschen	investigate (v)
erfüllen	accomplish (v)
ergänzen	amend (v)
Ergänzung	amendment (n)
Erhalten (is.v. einen Zustand erhalten)	maintain (v)
erhalten	obtain (v)
erhöhen (Chancen)	enhance (v)
erholen, sich	recover (v), recuperate (v), pick up (v)
Erlaubnis	permit (n)
Erlös	revenue (n)
ermüdet	weary (adj)
erreichen	accomplish (v), achieve (v), reach (v)
Erreichen	accomplishment (n)
Errungenschaft	achievement (n)
erschaffen	establish (v)
erweitern	broaden (v)
Etikett	label (n)
Expertenwissen	expertise (n)

F

Fachbuch	trade book (n)
Fachfrau, Fachmann	professional (n), expert
Fachzeitschrift	professional journal (n)
Fähigkeit	ability (n)
Fälle, für alle –	just in case (n)
falsch verbunden sein	have the wrong number (v)
Familienstand	marital status (n)
Ferngespräch	long-distance call (n)
Fernsehspitzenzeit	peak viewing (n)
Fertigkeit	skill (n)
Festnetz	landline
Festplatte	hard drive/disk (n)
Festschrift	commemorative brochure (n)
Flaggschiff	flagship (n)
Flugblatt	leaflet (n)
fluktuieren	fluctuate (v)
Folie (für OHP)	transparency (n)
Formatänderung	change in format (n)
Forschung	research (n)
Fragebogen	questionnaire (n)
Freizeichen	dialling tone (AE: dial tone) (n)

G

Gebühr	unit/charge (n)
Gehalt	salary (n)
Geheimnummer, eine – haben	be ex-directory (AE: have an unlisted number) (v)
Gelegenheit	opportunity (n)
genau	concise (adj), exact (adj)
Genauigkeit	accuracy (n)
Genehmigung	permit (n)
genügend	sufficient (adj)
Gerät	device (n)
Geschäftsführer	chief executive (n)
Geschäftsinteressent	stakeholder (n)

Geschäftskunde	professional customer (n)
gesund, bekömmlich	wholesome (adj)
Getränke	beverages (n)
getrennt werden	be disconnected (v)
gezielt suchen	scout (v)
gipfeln	culminate (v)
gleich bleiben	remain steady (v)
gleich bleiben, sich einpendeln	flatten out (v)
Gleichgesinnter	peer (n)
Grips	savvy (adj)
Großhandel	wholesale (n)
Großhändler; hier: Pressegrossist	wholesale trader (n)
gründen	found (v)
Gründer	founder (n)
gründlich	thorough (adj)
Grundstück	estate (n)
Grüße, jemandem freundliche – ausrichten	give somebody one's best wishes (v)

H

Haken	hook (n)
Handelsmarke	brand (n)
Handy	mobile phone (AE: cell phone) (n)
Handynummer	mobile number (AE: cell phone number) (n)
Handzeichen	show of hands (n)
Hauptversammlung	general meeting (n)
herantreten an	approach (v)
herbeiführen	encompass (v)
Herstellungsabteilung	production department (n)
herumgehen	mill around (v)
hervorbringen	spawn (v)
hervorrufen	evoke (v)
Hinweis	indication (n)
Hoch, ein – erreichen	reach a high/high-point (v)

hochschießen	shoot up (v), skyrocket (v)
Höhe, in die – schnellen	soar (v)
Höhepunkt, den – erreichen	culminate (v)
Hörer	receiver (n)
Hörer, den – auflegen	ring off (v)
Hörerschaft	audience (n)

I

Idee, eine – ablehnen	oppose an idea (v)
Inhalt	content (n)
Initiativbewerbung	exploratory application (n)
Innenrequisiteur	set dresser (n)
Inventar	inventory (n)

J

Jahreshauptver-sammlung	Annual General Meeting (n)
jonglieren	juggle (v)
justieren	adjust (v)

K

Kalkulation	estimating and costing (n)
Kamerabühne	dolly (n)
Kamerabühnenmann	grip (n)
Kameramann, lichtsetzender	director of photography (n)
Kameramann/-frau	camera operator (n)
Kampagne	campaign (n)
Karriere	career (n)
Kartentelefon	card phone (n)
Kasse	cash register (n)
Katalog	catalogue (n)
Katalogeintrag	catalogue data entry (n)
kaufen	acquire (v), purchase (v)
kaum	bare (adj), barely (adv)
Kenntnis	proficiency (n)
Kleidung	clothing (n)

Kleinanzeige	classified ad(vertisement) (n)
Klingelton	ringing tone (n)
Kollege	colleague (n)
Kollegium	staff (n)
kommunizieren	interact (v)
Konkurrenz	competition (n)
Konnotation	connotation (n)
Kontrolle, jemandem etwas zur – vorlesen	read something back to somebody (v)
Konzern	corporation (n)
Köpfchen	savvy (adj)
Kopfhörer mit Mikrofon	headset (n)
Korrekturen lesen	proof reading (n)
korrigieren	proofread (v)
Kostenschätzung	cost estimates (n)
kritisch, entscheidend	critical (adj)
kümmern, sich um etw. –	see to s.th. (v)
Kunde	client (n), patron (n), customer (n)
Kundendienstabteilung	customer service department (n)

L

Ländervorwahl	country code (n)
launchen	launch (v)
lauter sprechen	speak up (v)
Lautsprecher, jemanden auf – stellen	put somebody on loudspeaker (v)
Layout	layout (n)
lebensfähig	viable (adj)
Lebenslauf	Curriculum Vitae (CV) (n), (US: résumé (n))
Leiter, künstlerischer	art director (n)
Leitung, in der – bleiben	hold (v)
Leitung, Verbindung	line (n)
Lektoratsleitung, Redaktionsleitung	key editorial staff (n)

Leserschaft	audience (n)
Leuchtreklame	illuminated sign (n)
Lichttechniker	gaffer (n)
Linie, in erster –	primarily (adv)
Litfaßsäule	poster pillar (n)
Lizenz	license (n)
löschen, etwas –	delete something (v)
Lose-Blatt-Werk	loose-leaf-publication (n)

M

Management-	managerial (adj)
Marke	label (n), brand (n)
Markenartikel	branded goods (n)
Markentreue	brand loyalty (n)
Marketingkampagne	marketing campaign (n)
Markt, auf den – bringen	launch (v)
Marktforschung	market research (n)
Marktführer	market leader (n)
marktorientiert	market-driven (adj)
mäßig	moderate (adj)
Maximum, das – erreichen	reach a peak/maximum (v)
Mediaplaner	media planner (n)
Meeting, an einem – teilnehmen	attend a meeting (v)
Meeting, etwas zu einem – beitragen	contribute something to a meeting (v)
Mehrwert	added value (n)
melden, sich wieder bei jemandem –	get back to somebody (v)
merklich	marked (adj)
Merkmal	feature (n)
Mischpult	mixing board (n)
mitarbeiten	collaborate (v)
Mitarbeiter	employee (n)
Mitarbeiter, freier	freelancer (n)
Mitgefühl	empathy (n)
Mittel	means (n)

Motivsucher	location scout (n)
münden	result in (v)
Mundpropaganda	word-of-mouth (n)
Münztelefon	coin phone (n)
Muster	sample (n)
Muttersprachler	native speaker (n)

N

nachgewiesen	proven (adj)
Nachricht	message (n)
Nachricht, eine – hinterlassen	leave a message (v)
Nachricht, eine – notieren	take a message (v)
Nebenbedeutung	connotation (n)
Nebenstelle	extension (n)
Nichterscheinen am Arbeitsplatz	absenteeism (n)
Note (in der Schule)	grade (n)
notieren, etwas –	take something down (v)
notieren, sich etwas –	make a note of something (v)
Notruf	emergency call (n)
Nutzen	benefit (n)

O

Öffentlichkeitsarbeit	Public Relations (PR) (n)
Organigramm	organisation chart (n)
Ortsgespräch	local call (n)
Ortsvorwahl	dialling code (AE: area code) (n)

P

Palette	roster (n)
passen, jemandem –	suit somebody (v)
passend, etwas ist für jemanden – (z. B. Termin)	be convenient for somebody (v)

Personal	staff (n), personnel (n)
Personalabteilung	personnel department (n)
Personalchef	personnel director (n)
Personenkreis, erfasster – eines Mediums	coverage (n)
pflegen	maintain (v)
Piepser	pager (n)
Plakat	poster (n)
Planungsabteilung	strategic planning department (n)
Plattenfirma, große –	major label (n)
Plattenfirma, kleine, unabhängige –	independent label (n)
Plattenvertrag	recording contract (n)
plötzlich	sudden (adj), suddenly (adv)
PR (Public Relations)	Public Relations (PR) (n)
präzise	concise (adj)
Pressemitteilung	press release (n)
Priorität	priority (n)
Prioritätensetzung	prioritising (n)
Prioritäten setzen	prioritise (v)
Privatnummer	home number (n)
Produktionsassistent	production assistant (n)
produktiv	prolific (adj)
profitieren von	benefit from (v)
promoten	promote (v)
Prospekt	flyer (n)
Protokoll	minutes (n)
Protokoll, das – führen	take/keep the minutes (v)
Publicity	publicity (n)
Publikum	audience (n)
Punkt, den niedrigsten – erreichen	reach a minimum/lowest point (v)
Punkt, einen hohen – erreichen	reach a high/high-point (v)
Punkt, einen niedrigen – erreichen	reach/hit a low/low-point (v)

Q

Quelle	source (n)
Quorum (zur Beschlussfähigkeit vorgeschriebene Teilnehmerzahl)	quorum (n)

R

Raster	grid (n)
Redakteur	writer (n)
Redaktionsgeschäftsführer	editorial director (n)
Redaktionsleitung	key editorial staff (n)
Redigieren	editing skill (n)
Referenz, Bewerbung (i. S. v Person, die Auskunft über den Bewerber geben kann)	reference (n)
Referenz, Marketing (i. S. v berühmte Persönlichkeit, die für ein Produkt wirbt)	testimonial (n)
Regel	rule (n)
Regieassistent	assistant director (n)
Reklame	publicity (n)
rekrutieren	recruit (v)
Reporter	reporter (n)
Requisite	properties/props (n)
Requisiteur	prop master (n)
resultieren in	result in (v)
Rezept	recipe (v)
R-Gespräch	reverse charge call (n)
Risiko	threat (n)
Röhre	tube (n)

S

Schaum	froth (n)
Schauplatz	venue (n)
Schiene	track (n)
Schnittstellen	internal departments (n)
schnurloses (Telefon)	cordless phone (n)

Schriftart	font (n)
Schuld	guilt (n)
Schwäche	weakness (n)
schwanken	oscillate (v)
Schwerpunkt	focus (n)
Schwerpunkt setzen	dedicate (v)
Script/Continuity (Person, die auf Anschlüsse beim Filmdreh achtet)	continuity (n)
selten	rarely (adv), rare (adj)
senden	broadcast (v)
Sendung	broadcast (n)
sicherstellen	ensure (v)
Sichtfenster des Telefons	call display (n)
signieren	autograph (v)
Signierstunde	booksigning event (n)
solide	sound (adj)
Sonstiges	miscellaneous (n)
Spitze, eine – erreichen	reach a peak/maximum (v)
Spur	trace (n)
stabil bleiben	remain stable (v)
stabilisieren	stabilise (v)
Stadtverwaltung	town council (n)
Stärke	strength (n)
steigern	increase (v)
steil, jäh	steep (adj)
Stelle, freie	opening (n), vacancy (n)
Stellenanzeige	job advertisement (n)
stetig	steady (adj)
Stimme, entscheidende	deciding/casting vote (n)
Stimmung	mood (n)
Studienarbeit	thesis (n)
stürzen	plummet (v), slump (v)
synchronisieren (Film)	dub (v)

T

Tabellenkalkulation	spreadsheet (n)
Tages-Dispo	callsheet (n)

Tagesordnung	agenda (n)
Tagesordnung, die – verteilen	circulate the agenda (v)
Tagesordnung, eine – zusammenstellen	draw up an agenda (v)
Tagesordnungspunkt	item on the agenda (n)
Tagungsort	venue (n)
Talsohle	trough (adj)
Tantieme	royalty (n)
Tarif	rate (n)
tauschen	switch (v), exchange
Teilnehmer	participant (n)
Telefon, tragbarers	cordless phone (n)
Telefonauskunft	directory enquiries (AE: directory assistance) (n)
Telefonbuch	phone book/phone directory
Telefonhörer	receiver (n)
telefonisch	by phone (adj)
Telefonist(in)	operator, telephonist (n)
Telefonkarte	phone card (n)
Telefonkonferenz	conference call (n)
Telefonnummer	phone number (n)
Telefonverzeichnis	directory (n)
Telefonzelle	call box, phone box (AE: phone booth) (n)
Telefonzentrale	switchboard, exchange (n)
Termin	appointment (n)
Termin, einen – festmachen	fix an appointment (v)
Terminkalender	diary (AE: appointment book) (n)
Textilien	textiles (n)
Thema, ein – anschneiden, ein – ansprechen	raise a matter (v)
Tiefpunkt	trough (adj)
Titelübersicht	title list (n)
Toningenieur	recording engineer (n)
tragbar	portable (adj)

Treffpunkt	venue (n)
Tube	tube (n)

U

überblicken	oversee (v)
Überlegenheit	superiority (n)
überreden	persuade (v)
übertragen	convert (v), broadcast (v)
Übertragung	broadcast (n)
übertrieben	outlandish (adj)
überzeugend	convincing (adj)
umfassen, umgeben	encompass (v)
unerwartet	sudden (adj)
ungefähr	approximately
unmittelbar	immediate (adj)
Unterabteilung	subdivision (n)
Untergebener	subordinate (n)
unterscheiden	distinguish (v)
unterstellt, jdm. – sein	report to s. o. (v)
unterstützen	support (v)
Unterstützung (Marketing)	endorsement (n)
Untertitel	subtitles (n)
Untertitelung	subtitling (n)

V

Verabredung, private	date (n)
verantwortlich, für etwas – sein	responsible for, to be (v)
verbessern	amend (v), improve (v), enhance (v)
verbinden, jemanden mit jemandem/etwas –	connect somebody to somebody/something (v)
Verbindung	line (n)
Verbindung aufnehmen	liaise (v)
Verbindung, schlechte	bad line (n)
Verdauungs-	digestive (adj)
Verfasserbiografie	author profile (n)

Verfügung, zur – stellen	provide (v)
Verhaltenscodex, Verhaltensregeln	code of practise (n)
verhandeln	negotiate (v)
Verhandlung	negotiation (n)
Verkäufer	vendor (n)
Verkaufsauflage	circulation (n)
Verkaufswerbung	sales promotion (n)
Verlag	publishing company (n)
vermeiden	avoid (n)
vermitteln	convey (v)
Vermittlung	operator, telephonist (n)
Veröffentlichung	publication (n)
Verpackung	packaging (n)
Versammlung, Fragen an die – weiterleiten	refer questions to the floor (v)
Versand nach Katalogen	mail order (n)
Verschiedenes	any other business (AOB) (n)
verschwinden	disappear (v)
Versicherung	insurance (n)
verstärken	strengthen (v)
Vertrag	contract (n)
vertraulich	confidential (adj)
Vertrieb	distribution (n)
Vertriebsabteilung	distribution department (n)
verwählen, sich	dial a wrong number (v)
Verwaltung	administration (n)
Vieh	livestock (n)
Vielfalt	diversity (n), variety (n)
Volkswirtschaftslehre	economics (n)
Vollendung	accomplishment (n)
Vorgehensweise	procedure (n)
Vorgesetzter	superior (n)
Vorlesen, Vorspielen (beim Film/Theater)	prereading (n)
vormerken, sich etwas –	pencil something in (v)
Vorschlag	proposal (n)

Vorsitz, den – bei einem Meeting haben	chair a meeting (v)
Vorsitzender	chairperson (n)
Vorstandsvorsitzender	CEO – Chief Executive Officer (n)
Vorteil	benefit (n)
Vorwahl	code (n)
Vorwahl, internationale	international (access) code (n)

W

wachsen	grow (v)
wählen	dial (v)
Warenzeichen	trademark (n)
Warteschleife, jemanden in die – schalten	put somebody on hold (v)
wechseln	switch (v)
wecken (z. B. Bedürfnis)	arouse (v)
Weisungskette	chain of command (n)
Werbeagentur	advertising agency (n)
Werbeanzeige	advertisement/advert/ad (n)
Werbebrief	direct mail (n)
Werbebroschüre	booklet (n)
Werbefeldzug, einen – durchführen	run a campaign (v)
Werbegeschenk	giveaway (n)
werben, jemanden	recruit (v)
Werbetafel	billboard (n)
Werbetext	copy (n)
Werbetexter	copy writer (n)
Werbetrick	gimmick (n)
Werbung	promotion (n)
Werbung (als Branche, Oberbegriff)	advertising (n)
Werbung, (insbes. TV-Werbung)	commercial (n) (US)
Werbungtreibender	advertiser (n)
Werdegang	career (n)

Werkzeug, Methode	tool (n)
Wert	value (n)
wesentlich	substantial (adj)
Wettbewerb	competition (n)
Wettbewerb, im – stehen	compete (v)
wettbewerbsfähig	competitive (adj)
wieder ansteigen	pick up (v)
wiederholen, etwas –	read something back (v)
Wiederverkäufer	reseller (n)
wiederverschließbar	resealable (adj)
wohltätig	charitable (adj)
Wort, das – ergreifen	take the floor (v)
Wort, sich zu – melden	raise one's hand (v)
Wortspiel	pun (n)

X

Y

Z

Zeitschrift	magazine (n)
Zeitung	newspaper (n)
Zertifikat, Zeugnis	certificate (n)
Ziel	objective (n), goal (n),
zielen auf	aim at (v)
Zielgruppe	target group (n)
zuarbeiten	support (v)
zufällig	fortuitous
Zugänglichkeit	accessibility (n)
zurückrufen, jemanden –	call somebody back (v), return somebody's call
zusammenarbeiten, mit jdm.	liaise with s. o. (v)
zusammenarbeiten	collaborate (v)
zusammenfassen	sum up (v)
zusammenfassen, etwas –	sum something up (v), summarise something (v)

zuschneiden, etwas – auf	tailor s. th. to (v)
zuständig, für etwas – sein	charge of, to be in (v)

English – German

A

A&R representative (n)	A&R Manager (Musikbusiness)
ability (n)	Fähigkeit
abroad (adj)	im Ausland
absenteeism (n)	Nichterscheinen am Arbeitsplatz
abstain from a vote (v)	sich einer Abstimmung enthalten
accept an objection (v)	einem Einwand stattgeben
accessibility (n)	Zugänglichkeit
accomplish (v)	erfüllen, erreichen
accomplishment (n)	Vollendung, Erreichen
account executive (n)	Chefbuchhalter
accountant (n)	Buchhalter
accounts department (n)	Buchhaltungsabteilung
accuracy (n)	Genauigkeit
achieve (v)	erreichen
achievement (n)	Errungenschaft
acquire (v)	akquirieren, kaufen, anschaffen
acquisition (n)	Akquise, Anschaffung
added value (n)	Mehrwert
adjust (v)	einstellen, justieren
administration (n)	Verwaltung
advertisement/advert/ad (n)	Werbung, Werbeanzeige
advertiser (n)	Werbungtreibender
advertising (n)	Werbung (als Branche, Oberbegriff)
advertising agency (n)	Werbeagentur
advertising brief (n)	Anweisungen/Briefing zu einer Werbekampagne

advertising department (n)	Anzeigenabteilung
advise (v)	beraten
agenda (n)	Tagesordnung
aim at (v)	zielen auf
amend (v)	ergänzen, verbessern
amendment (n)	Änderung, Ergänzung
Annual General Meeting (n)	Jahreshauptversammlung
abstention (n)	Enthaltung
answer a call (v)	einen Anruf entgegennehmen
answering machine, answerphone (n)	Anrufbeantworter
any other business (AOB) (n)	Verschiedenes
appeal to (v)	appellieren, ansprechen
applicant (n)	Bewerber
application (n)	Bewerbung, Anwendung
appointment (n)	Termin
approach (v)	herantreten an
appropriate (adj)	angemessen
approximately (adv)	ungefähr
arouse (v)	wecken (z. B. Bedürfnis)
arrange a meeting (v)	einen Besprechungstermin festlegen
art director (n)	Art Director, künstlerischer Leiter
articulate (v)	klar ausdrücken
artwork (n)	Artwork (z. B. Zeichnungen, Fotos, die zu Werbezwecken verwendet werden)
assess (v)	einschätzen, bewerten
assistant director (n)	Regieassistent
attach (v)	beifügen, anhängen
attachment (n)	Anlage, Anhang
attend a meeting (v)	an einem Meeting teilnehmen
attract (v)	anziehen

audience (n)	Hörer-/Leserschaft, Publikum
author profile (n)	Verfasserbiografie
autograph (v)	signieren
avoid (n)	vermeiden

B

bad line (n)	schlechte Verbindung
bare (adj)	kaum
be a quorum (v)	beschlussfähig sein
be convenient for somebody (v)	etwas ist für jemanden passend (z. B. Termin)
be disconnected (v)	getrennt werden
be ex-directory (AE: have an unlisted number) (v)	eine Geheimnummer haben
be in favour of (v)	dafür sein
benefit (n)	Vorteil, Nutzen
benefit from (v)	profitieren von
best boy (n)	Assistent (Beleuchtung, Bühne)
beverages (n)	Getränke
billboard (n)	Werbetafel
booklet (n)	Werbebroschüre
booksigning event (n)	Signierstunde
brand (n)	Handelsmarke, Marke
brand loyalty (n)	Markentreue
branded goods (n)	Markenartikel
broadcast (n)	Übertragung, Sendung
broadcast (v)	übertragen, senden
broaden (v)	erweitern
business studies (n)	Betriebswirtschafts-lehre
busy (AE) (adj)	besetzt
busy signal (n)	Besetztzeichen
by phone (adj)	telefonisch

C

call (n)	Anruf
call/make a call (v)	anrufen

call box (n)	Telefonzelle
call display (n)	Sichtfenster des Telefons
call for tenders (v)	eine Ausschreibung machen
call somebody (v)	jemanden anrufen
call somebody back (v)	jemanden zurückrufen
callsheet (n)	(Tages-)Dispo
camera operator (n)	Kameramann/-frau
campaign (n)	Kampagne
cancel a meeting (v)	eine Besprechung absagen
caption (n)	Bildunterschrift
carbon copy (n)	Durchschlag
card phone (n)	Kartentelefon
career (n)	Karriere, Werdegang
carry a motion (v)	einen Antrag annehmen
cash register (n)	Kasse
casting director (n)	Caster
catalogue data entry (n)	Katalogeintrag
catalogue (n)	Katalog
cell phone (AE)	Handy
cell phone number (AE)	Handynummer
CEO – Chief Executive Officer (n)	Vorstandsvorsitzender
certificate (n)	Zertifikat, Zeugnis
chain of command (n)	Weisungskette
chair a meeting (v)	den Vorsitz bei einem Meeting haben
chairperson (n)	Vorsitzender, Vorsitzende
change in format (n)	Formatänderung
charge of, to be in (v)	für etwas zuständig sein
charitable (adj)	wohltätig
cherrypicker (n)	Bockkran
chief executive (n)	Geschäftsführer
Chief Executive Officer (n)	Vorstandsvorsitzender
circulate the agenda (v)	die Tagesordnung verteilen
circulation (n)	(Verkaufs-)Auflage
classified ad(vertisement) (n)	Kleinanzeige

client (n)	Kunde
code (n)	Vorwahl
code of practice (n)	Verhaltenscodex, -regeln
coin phone (n)	Münztelefon
collaborate (v)	zusammenarbeiten, mitarbeiten
colleague (n)	Kollege
commemorative brochure (n)	Festschrift
commercial (n)	Werbung, insbes. TV-Werbung (US)
commit (v)	anbinden
commitment (n)	Bereitschaft, Engagement
committee meeting (n)	Ausschusssitzung
compete (v)	im/in Wettbewerb stehen
competition (n)	Wettbewerb, Konkurrenz
competitive (adj)	wettbewerbsfähig
concise (adj)	genau, präzise
conference call (n)	Telefonkonferenz
confidential (adj)	vertraulich
confirm something (v)	etwas bestätigen
connect somebody to somebody/ something (v)	jemanden mit jemandem/ etwas verbinden
connotation (n)	Konnotation, Nebenbedeutung
consist of (v)	bestehen aus
constraint (n)	Beschränkung, Einschränkung
consult (v)	beraten
content (n)	Inhalt
continuity (n)	Script/Continuity (Person, die auf Anschlüsse beim Filmdreh achtet)
contract (n)	Vertrag
contribute (v)	beitragen
contribute something to a meeting (v)	etwas zu einem Meeting beitragen
convert (v)	übertragen
convey (v)	vermitteln

convincing (adj)	überzeugend
copy (n)	Werbetext
copy writer (n)	Werbetexter
cordless phone (n)	schnurloses/tragbares Telefon
corporation (n)	Konzern
cost estimates (n)	Kostenschätzung
country code (n)	Ländervorwahl
cover letter (n)	(Bewerbungs)anschreiben
coverage (n)	erfasster Personenkreis eines Mediums
critical (adj)	kritisch, entscheidend
culminate (v)	gipfeln, den Höhepunkt erreichen
Curriculum Vitae (CV) (n)	Lebenslauf
customer (n)	Kunde
customer service department (n)	Kundendienst-abteilung

D

date (n)	private Verabredung
deciding/casting vote (n)	entscheidende Stimme
decline (v), decrease (v)	abnehmen
dedicate (v)	Schwerpunkt setzen
defeat a motion (v)	einen Antrag ablehnen
degree (n)	Abschluss (Schule, Uni)
delete something (v)	etwas löschen
department (n)	Abteilung
deployment (n)	Anwendung, Einsatz
derive from (v)	ableiten von
design studio (n)	Layout
device (n)	Gerät, Apparat
dial (v)	wählen
dial a wrong number (v)	sich verwählen
dialling code (AE: area code) (n)	Ortsvorwahl
dialling tone (AE: dial tone) (n)	Freizeichen

diary (AE: appointment book) (n)	Terminkalender
digestive (adj)	Verdauungs-
digress (v)	abschweifen
diminish (v)	verschwinden
direct line (n)	Durchwahl
direct mail (n)	Werbebrief
director of photography (n)	lichtsetzender Kameramann
directory (n)	Telefonverzeichnis
directory enquiries (AE: directory assistance) (n)	Telefonauskunft
disciplinary action (n)	Disziplinarmaßnahmen
dismissal (n)	Entlassung
display ad(vertisement) (n)	gestaltete Anzeige
distinguish (v)	unterscheiden
distribution (n)	Vertrieb
distribution department (n)	Vertriebsabteilung
diversity (n)	Vielfalt
division of labour (n)	Arbeitsteilung
dolly (n)	Dolly, Kamerabühne
draw up an agenda (v)	eine Tagesordnung zusammenstellen
drop (v)	abfallen
drop a motion (v)	einen Antrag fallen lassen
dub (v)	synchronisieren (Film)

E

economics (n)	Volkswirtschaftslehre
editing skill (n)	Redigieren
editor (n)	Chefredakteur
editorial director (n)	Redaktionsgeschäftsführer
emergency call (n)	Notruf
empathy (n)	Mitgefühl, Einfühlungsvermögen
emphasise (v)	betonen
employ (v)	anstellen, beschäftigen

employee (n)	Mitarbeiter, Angestellter
employer (n)	Arbeitgeber
encompass (v)	umgeben, umfassen, herbeiführen
endeavor (n)	Bemühen
endorsement (n)	Unterstützung, Marketing
engaged (BE) (adj)	besetzt
engaged tone (AE: busy signal) (n)	Besetztzeichen
enhance (v)	verbessern, erhöhen (Chancen)
ensure (v)	absichern, sicherstellen
enthusiasm (n)	Begeisterung
escort (v)	begleiten
establish (v)	aufbauen, erschaffen
estate (n)	Grundstück
estimating and costing (n)	Kalkulation
evaluate (v)	bewerten
evoke (v)	hervorrufen
exchange (n)	Telefonzentrale
expand (v)	ausweiten
expert (n)	Fachfrau, -mann
expertise (n)	Expertenwissen
exploratory application (n)	Initiativbewerbung
extension (n)	Durchwahl, Nebenstelle

F

fall (v)	abfallen, abnehmen
feature (n)	Merkmal
fix a meeting (v)	einen Besprechungstermin festlegen, eine Besprechung ansetzen
fix an appointment (v)	einen Termin fest- machen
flagship (n)	Flaggschiff, Aushängeschild
flatten out (v)	gleich bleiben, sich einpendeln
fluctuate (v)	fluktuieren
flyer (n)	Prospekt

focus (n)	Schwerpunkt
font (n)	Schriftart
foray (n)	Beutezug
fortuitous	zufällig
found (v)	gründen
founder (n)	Gründer
freelancer (n)	freier Mitarbeiter
freeze on recruitment (n)	Einstellungsstopp
froth (n)	Schaum

G

gaffer (n)	Lichttechniker
gear to (v)	ausrichten auf
general meeting (n)	Hauptversammlung
genre fiction (n)	Belletristik
get back to somebody (v)	sich wieder bei jemandem melden
gimmick (n)	Werbetrick, Attraktion
give somebody a message (v)	jemandem etwas ausrichten
give somebody one's best wishes (v)	jemandem freundliche Grüße ausrichten
giveaway (n)	Werbegeschenk
go down (v)	abnehmen, abfallen
go up (v)	ansteigen
goal (n)	Ziel
grab someones attention (v)	die Aufmerksamkeit von jdm. erlangen
grade (n)	(Schul-)note
grid (n)	Raster
grip (n)	Kamerabühnenmann
grow (v)	wachsen, ansteigen
guilt (n)	Schuld

H

hang up (v)	auflegen
hard drive/disk (n)	Festplatte

have a meeting (v)	eine Besprechung abhalten
have the wrong number (v)	falsch verbunden sein
head of department (n)	Abteilungsleiter
headset (n)	Kopfhörer mit Mikrofon
hit the shelf (v)	ausgeliefert sein
hold (v)	in der Leitung bleiben
hold a meeting (v)	eine Besprechung abhalten
hold all calls (v)	keine Anrufe durchstellen
home number (n)	Privatnummer
hook (n)	Haken, Aufhänger

I

illuminated sign (n)	Leuchtreklame
immediate (adj)	unmittelbar
impact (n)	Effekt, Auswirkung
improve (v)	verbessern
incoming call (adj)	eingehender Anruf
increase (v)	ansteigen, steigern
independent label (n)	kleine, unabhängige Plattenfirma
indication (n)	Anzeichen, Hinweis
insert (n)	Beilage
insurance (n)	Versicherung
interact (v)	kommunizieren
interchangeably (adv)	austauschbar
internal departments (n)	Schnittstellen
international (access) code (n)	internationale Vorwahl
interview (n)	Befragung
inventory (n)	Inventar
investigate (v)	erforschen
item on the agenda (n)	Tagesordnungspunkt

J

jacket copy (n)	Klappen-/Umschlagtext
job advertisement (n)	Stellenanzeige

Vocabulary

job application (n)	Bewerbung
job interview (n)	Bewerbungsgespräch
juggle (v)	jonglieren
just in case (n)	für alle Fälle

K

keep the minutes (v)	das Protokoll führen
key editorial staff (n)	Lektoratsleitung, Redaktionsleitung

L

label (n)	Etikett, Marke
landline (n)	Festnetz
launch (n)	Einführung (Markt)
launch (v)	auf den Markt bringen, einführen, launchen
leaflet (n)	Flugblatt
leave a message (v)	eine Nachricht hinterlassen
level off (v)	sich einpendeln
liaise (v)	Verbindung aufnehmen
liaise with s. o. (v)	mit jdm. zusammen arbeiten
license (n)	Lizenz
lighting (n)	Beleuchtung
line (n)	Leitung, Verbindung
literate (adj)	bewandert (i.S.v. sich mit etw. gut auskennen)
livestock (n)	Vieh
local call (n)	Ortsgespräch
location manager (n)	Aufnahmeleiter
location scout (n)	Motivsucher
long-distance call (n)	Ferngespräch
loose-leaf-publication (n)	Lose-Blatt-Werk

M

magazine (n)	Zeitschrift
mail order (n)	(Katalog)-Versand

maintain (v)	erhalten, pflegen
major label (n)	große Plattenfirma
make a note of something (v)	sich etwas notieren
managerial (adj)	Management-
marital status (n)	Familienstand
marked (adj)	deutlich, merklich, ausgeprägt
market leader (n)	Marktführer
market research (n)	Marktforschung
market-driven (adj)	marktorientiert
marketing campaign (n)	Marketingkampagne
means (n)	Mittel
media buyer (n)	Mediaeinkäufer
media planner (n)	Mediaplaner
message (n)	Nachricht
mill around (v)	herumgehen
minutes (n)	Protokoll
miscellaneous (n)	Sonstiges
mixing board (n)	Mischpult
mobile number (n)	Handynummer
mobile phone (n)	Handy
moderate (adj)	mäßig
mood (n)	Stimmung
motion (n)	Antrag

N

native speaker (n)	Muttersprachler
need (n)	Bedürfnis
negotiate (v)	verhandeln
negotiation (n)	Verhandlung
newspaper (n)	Zeitung
notes, records (n)	Aufzeichnungen

O

objective (n)	Ziel
obtain (v)	erhalten

officemate (n)	Bürokollege
omit (v)	auslassen
opening (n)	freie Stelle
operate (v)	bedienen
operator (n)	Vermittlung, Telefonist(in)
opportunity (n)	Gelegenheit, Chance
oppose an idea (v)	eine Idee ablehnen
organisation chart (n)	Organigramm
oscillate (v)	schwanken
outgoing call (adj)	abgehender Anruf
outlandish (adj)	übertrieben
overrule an objection (v)	einen Einwand zurückweisen
oversee (v)	überblicken

P

packaging (n)	Verpackung
pager (n)	Piepser
participant (n)	Teilnehmer
pass a motion (v)	einen Antrag annehmen
patron (n)	Kunde
peak viewing (n)	Fernsehspitzenzeit
peer (n)	Gleichgesinnter
pencil something in (v)	sich etwas vormerken
permit (n)	Erlaubnis, Genehmigung
personnel (n)	Personal
personnel department (n)	Personalabteilung
personnel director (n)	Personalchef
persuade (v)	überreden
phone book/phone directory	Telefonbuch
phone booth (AE), phone box (n)	Telefonzelle
phone card (n)	Telefonkarte
phone number (n)	Telefonnummer
pick up (v)	wieder ansteigen, sich erholen

pitch (n)	hier: Runde von mehreren um einen Auftrag konkurrierenden Agenturen
pitch-perimeter advertising (n)	Bandenwerbung
plummet (v)	stürzen
properties/props (n)	Requisite
portable (adj)	tragbar
poster (n)	Plakat
poster pillar (n)	Litfaßsäule
postpone a meeting (v)	eine Besprechung verschieben
prereading (n)	Vorlesen, Vorspielen (beim Film/Theater)
press release (n)	Pressemitteilung
primarily (adv)	in erster Linie
print buying (n)	Auftragsvergabe
print product (n)	Druckerzeugnis
prioritise (v)	Prioritäten setzen
prioritising (n)	Prioritätensetzung
priority (n)	Priorität
procedure (n)	Vorgehensweise
process (v)	bearbeiten
production assistant (n)	Produktionsassistent
production department (n)	Herstellungsabteilung
professional (n)	Berufstätige(r), Fachfrau/-mann
professional customer (n)	Geschäftskunde
professional journal (n)	Fachzeitschrift
proficiency (n)	Kenntnis
prolific (adj)	produktiv
promote (v)	befördern, promoten
promotion (n)	Werbung
proofreading (n)	das Korrekturlesen
proofread (v)	korrigieren
prop master (n)	Requisiteur
proposal (n)	Vorschlag
propose a motion (v)	einen Antrag stellen
protect (v)	beschützen

proven (adj)	nachgewiesen
provide (v)	zur Verfügung stellen
Public Relations (PR) (n)	Öffentlichkeitsarbeit, PR
publication (n)	Veröffentlichung
publicity (n)	Publicity, Reklame
publishing company (n)	Verlag
pun (n)	Wortspiel
purchase (v)	erwerben, (ein-)kaufen
put somebody on hold (v)	jemanden in die Warteschleife schalten
put somebody on loudspeaker (v)	jemanden auf Lautsprecher stellen
put somebody through (to somebody) (v)	jemanden (zu jemandem) durchstellen

Q

questionnaire (n)	Fragebogen
quorum (n)	Quorum, zur Beschlussfähigkeit vorgeschriebene Teilnehmerzahl

R

raise a matter (v)	ein Thema ansprechen, anschneiden
raise objections (v)	Einwände erheben
raise one's hand (v)	sich zu Wort melden
rarely (adv)	selten
rate (n)	Tarif
reach a consensus (v)	eine Einigung erzielen
reach a high/high-point (v)	ein Hoch/einen hohen Punkt erreichen
reach a minimum (v)	den niedrigsten Punkt erreichen
reach a peak/maximum (v)	eine Spitze/das Maximum erreichen
reach/hit a low/low-point (v)	einen niedrigen Punkt erreichen
read something back (v)	etwas wiederholen
read something back to somebody (v)	jemandem etwas zur Kontrolle vorlesen

reasoning (n)	logisches Denken
receiver (n)	*Telefonhörer*
recipe (v)	Rezept
recommendable (adj)	empfehlenswert
recommendation (n)	Empfehlung
recording contract (n)	Plattenvertrag
recording engineer (n)	Toningenieur
recording gear (n)	Aufnahmezubehör
recover (v)	sich erholen
recruit (v)	rekrutieren, (jdn.) werben
recruiter (n)	(Personal)anwerber
recuperate (v)	sich erholen
refer questions to the floor (v)	Fragen an die Versammlung weiterleiten
reference (n)	Referenz, Bewerbung (i. S. v. Person, die Auskunft über den Bewerber geben kann.)
reject a motion (v)	einen Antrag ablehnen
relationship (n)	Beziehung
remain stable (v)	stabil bleiben
remain steady (v)	gleich bleiben
report to s. o. (v)	jdm. unterstellt sein
reporter (n)	Reporter
request (v)	anfragen, anfordern
resealable (adj)	wiederverschließbar
research (n)	Forschung
reseller (n)	Wiederverkäufer
resolution (n)	Beschluss, Auflösung (z. B. beim Monitor)
responsible for, to be (v)	für etwas verantwortlich sein
result in (v)	münden/resultieren in
résumé (n)	Lebenslauf (AE)
retail (n)	Einzelhandel
retail outlet (n)	Einzelhandelsgeschäft
retailer	Einzelhändler
return somebody's call (v)	jemanden zurückrufen
revenue (n)	Erlös, Einkommen

reverse charge call (n)	R-Gespräch
ring off (v)	den Hörer auflegen
ring somebody (v)	jemanden anrufen
ringing tone (n)	Klingelton
rise (v)	ansteigen
roam (v)	stöbern
roam through (v)	durchstöbern
roster (n)	Liste, Plan (AE), hier: Palette
royalty (n)	Tantieme
rule (n)	Regel
run a campaign (v)	einen Werbefeldzug durchführen

S

salary (n)	Gehalt
sales promotion (n)	Verkaufswerbung
sample (n)	Muster
savvy (adj)	Grips, Köpfchen
schedule/set up a meeting (v)	eine Besprechung ansetzen
scout (v)	(gezielt) suchen
script (n)	Drehbuch
script breakdown (n)	Drehbuchauszüge
second a motion (v)	einen Antrag unterstützen
secret ballot (n)	geheime Abstimmung
see to s. th. (v)	sich um etw. kümmern
self-assess (v)	sich selbst bewerten
set dresser (n)	Innenrequisiteur
sharp (adj)	deutlich
shelve a motion (v)	einen Antrag zurückstellen
shoot up (v)	hochschießen
shooting (n)	Dreh
shooting schedule (n)	Drehplan
shot (n)	Aufnahme
show of hands (n)	Handzeichen
similarity (n)	Ähnlichkeit
skill (n)	Fertigkeit

skyrocket (v)	hochschießen
slide (n)	Dia, Folie (bei Powerpoint-Präsentation)
slump (v)	stürzen, abrutschen
soar (v)	in die Höhe schnellen
sound (adj)	solide
source (n)	Quelle
spawn (v)	hervorbringen
speak up (v)	lauter sprechen
speaking	„am Apparat“
spell something (v)	etwas buchstabieren
spreadsheet (n)	Tabellenkalkulation
stabilise (v)	stabilisieren
staff (n)	Personal, Belegschaft, Kollegium
stage (n)	Bühne
stakeholder (n)	Geschäftsinteressent, Anteilsnehmer, Betroffener
stay at the same level (v)	auf einem Niveau bleiben
stay on the line (v)	am Apparat bleiben
steady (adj)	stetig
steep (adj)	steil, jäh
strapline (n)	
strategic planning (n)	Planungsabteilung
strength (n)	Stärke
strengthen (v)	ausbauen, verstärken
sub editor (n)	Chef vom Dienst
subdivision (n)	Unterabteilung
subordinate (n)	Untergebener
subscription (n)	Abonnement
subsequent (adj)	aufeinanderfolgend
subscription service (n)	Abonnement-Service
substantial (adj)	beträchtlich, wesent- lich
subtitles (n)	Untertitel
subtitling (n)	Untertitelung
sudden (adj)	unerwartet, plötzlich
suffice (v)	ausreichen

sufficient (adj)	genügend, ausreichend
suit somebody (v)	jemandem passen
sum something up (v)	etwas zusammenfassen
sum up (v)	zusammenfassen
summarise something (v)	etwas zusammenfassen
superior (n)	Vorgesetzter
superiority (n)	Überlegenheit
support (v)	unterstützen, zuarbeiten
survey (n)	Befragung
switch (v)	wechseln, tauschen
switchboard (n)	Telefonzentrale

T

tailor s. th. to (v)	etwas zuschneiden auf
take a call (v)	einen Anruf entgegennehmen
take a message (v)	eine Nachricht notieren
take a vote (v)	eine Abstimmung vornehmen
take part in a meeting (v)	an einer Besprechung teilnehmen
take something down (v)	etwas notieren
take sth. as read (v)	etwas als bekannt voraussetzen
take the floor (v)	das Wort ergreifen
take the minutes (v)	das Protokoll führen
target group (n)	Zielgruppe
telephone book (n), telephone directory (n)	Telefonbuch
telephonist (n)	Vermittlung, Telefonist(in)
testimonial (n)	Referenz, Marketing (i. S. v. berühmte Persönlichkeit, die für ein Produkt wirbt)
that's fine by me (v)	Das passt mir gut.
thesis (n)	Studienarbeit, Diplomarbeit
thorough (adj)	gründlich
threat (n)	Bedrohung, Risiko
title list (n)	Titelübersicht

to be promoted	befördert werden
tool (n)	Werkzeug, Methode
town council (n)	Stadtverwaltung
trace (n)	Spur
track (n)	Schiene
trade book (n)	Fachbuch
trademark (n)	Warenzeichen
trainee (n)	Auszubildende/r
transparency (n)	Folie (für OHP)
trial and error (n)	Versuch und Irrtum
trough (adj)	Tiefpunkt, Talsohle
tube (n)	Tube, Röhre (London auch: U-Bahn)

U

unanimous (adj)	einstimmig
unique (adj)	einzigartig
unit/charge (n)	Einheit/Gebühr
unveil (v)	enthüllen
urgent (adj)	dringend
userfriendliness (n)	Anwenderfreundlichkeit
utmost (adj)	äußerst

V

vacancy (n)	freie Stelle
value (n)	Wert
variety (n)	Vielfalt
vendor (n)	Verkäufer
venue (n)	Schauplatz, Austragungsort, Tagungsort, Treffpunkt
viable (adj)	lebensfähig
voicemail (n)	Anrufbeantworter

W

weakness (n)	Schwäche
weary (adj)	ermüdet
wholesale (n)	Großhandel

wholesale trader (n)	Großhändler; hier: Pressegrossist
wholesome (adj)	gesund, bekömmlich
word-of-mouth (n)	Mundpropaganda
work number (n)	Büronummer
writer (n)	Redakteur

y

yellow pages (n)	Branchenverzeichnis

Pronunciation and phonetic symbols

As you know by now, there are no simple rules for spelling in English. Also, the way a word is written does not always show you how to say it.
Dictionaries use special symbols and marks to show how words are pronounced and which syllable has the main stress. In most dictionaries, the symbols are based on a system known as the International Phonetic Alphabet (IPA).
The letters of the IPA are known as phonetic symbols because they represent sounds. Some are pronounced the way they are written, e. g. [m] for **m**oney and [l] for **l**ots. Others may not be what you expect, e. g. [j] for **y**et and **y**olk, and [d_3] for **j**et and **j**oke.
On the next page is a list of sounds included in the IPA, with examples of words containing these sounds. Dictionaries usually give a key to symbols, but it is worth learning the basic system anyway.

Consonants

b	(**b**ig, **b**ack, **bubb**le)
d	(**d**i**d**, **d**og, **dadd**y)
f	(**f**all, **ph**one, enou**gh**)
g	(**g**o, tar**g**et, jo**gg**ing)
h	(**h**at, **h**ouse, be**h**ind)
j	(**y**es, on**i**on, vign**e**tte)
k	(**k**ey, **c**li**ck**, **ch**emist)
l	(**l**ot, **l**eg, ye**ll**ow)
m	(**m**oney, so**me**, cli**mb**)
n	(**n**o, **kn**ow, **n**i**n**e)
p	(**p**ig, o**p**en, o**pp**osite)
r	(**r**ed, **r**ing, ca**rr**y)
s	(**s**ee, **s**ix, **sc**ien**c**e)
t	(**t**oo, **t**wo, a**tt**raction)
v	(**v**ideo, **v**an, e**v**ent)
w	(**w**et, **w**on, **o**ne)
z	(**z**ip, **z**ero, i**s**, ea**s**y)
dʒ	(**j**am, a**g**enda, **j**u**dg**e, sol**di**er)
ʃ	(**sh**ip, **s**ugar, mi**ss**ion, ac**t**ion)
θ	(**th**ree, **th**ick, **th**roat)
ð	(**th**e, **th**at, **th**ese)
tʃ	(**ch**eck, lun**ch**, a**ch**ieve, na**t**ure)
ʒ	(clo**s**ure, vi**s**ion, mea**s**ure, inva**s**ion)
ŋ	(si**ng**, lo**ng**, ha**ng**, to**ngue**)

Syllable stress

ˈ syllable with the main stress e. g. ˈʌndə (<u>un</u>der)

ˌ syllable with the secondary stress (plus main stress) e. g. ˌʌnˈduː (un<u>do</u>)

Short vowels

ɪ	s**i**t, b**u**sy, pock**e**t, w**o**men	
e	t**e**n, b**e**d, s**ai**d	
æ	c**a**t, b**a**d, p**a**ttern	
ʌ	r**u**n, fl**oo**d, s**o**n, r**ou**gh	
ɒ	h**o**t, w**a**sh, l**o**t	(BE)
ʊ	p**u**t, g**oo**d, sh**ou**ld, w**o**man	
ə	th**e, a**lone, col**ou**r, curi**ou**s	
i	happ**y**, cos**y**, funn**y**, prett**y**	
u	infl**u**ence, sit**u**ation, act**u**al	

Long vowels

iː	s**ee**, t**ea**, rec**ei**ve, l**ea**ve	
ɑː	he**ar**t, st**ar**t, **ar**m, p**ar**k	(BE/AE)
	h**o**t, w**a**sh, l**o**t	(AE)
ɔː	s**aw**, fl**oo**r, n**or**th, w**ar**	
ɜː	b**ur**n, g**ir**l, l**ear**n, n**ur**se	(BE)
ɜː(r)	b**ur**n, g**ir**l, l**ear**n, n**ur**se	(AE)

Diphthongs

eɪ	d**a**y, f**a**ce, p**ai**d, m**a**de	
aɪ	sk**y**, h**igh**, **I**'ll, **ai**sle	
ɔɪ	b**oy**, c**oi**n, ch**oi**ce	
əʊ	g**o**, l**ow**, d**ou**gh	(BE)
oʊ	g**o**, l**ow**, gr**ow**, d**ou**gh	(AE)
aʊ	h**ow**, h**ou**se, l**ou**d, cr**ow**d	
ɪə	n**ear**, we'**re**, b**eer**, t**ier**	(BE)
eə	h**air**, w**ear**, squ**are**, c**are**	(BE)
ʊə	s**ure**, r**ur**al, j**ur**y	
aɪə	b**uyer**, h**igher**, f**ire**, l**iar**	
aʊə	s**our**, fl**our**, fl**ower**	

BE: British English
AE: American English
consonant: Mitlaut/Konsonant, vowel: Selbstlaut/Vokal, diphthong: Doppellaut/Diphthong

Pronunciation and accents

Your **accent** is the way you pronounce words. It can show your regional background (an Australian accent, a Scottish accent) and even your social status (a posh accent, a common accent). **Received pronunciation (RP)** is the regionally neutral accent used by many middle class speakers in England. The American equivalent is known as **General American (GA)**. Some words are pronounced differently in RP and GA, for example:

Examples	**RP**	**GA**
th**ough**t, c**au**ght	[ɔ] as in c**o**re	[ɑː] as in c**a**r
wri**t**er, me**t**al	[**t**] as in **t**op	[d] **as** in ri**d**er
d**u**ty, n**ew**	[jʊ] as in b**eauty**, **you**	[uː] as in m**oo**dy, bl**ue**
hai**r** ca**r**e, bea**r**	[eə] silent 'R'	[er] voiced 'R'

Bildquellenverzeichnis

akg-images: S. 88
Fotolia: S. 7 (Yuri Arcurs), 8 (Tomasz Trojanowski), 10 (Franz Pflügl), 13 (raven), 15 (Vladimir Melnikov), 17 (Yuri Arcurs), 18 (Amir Kaljikovic), 19 (Monkey Business), 19 (nyul), 20 (endostock), 24 (Feng Yu), 26 (moonrun), 26 (Peter Göbel), 30 (Falko Matte), 31 (Rtimages), 36 (Yuri Arcurs), 38 (ArTo), 40 (felixbruno), 41 (Kenneth Sponsler), 42 (Maria P.), 43 (Fatman 73), 45 (Andres Roddriguez), 47 (Artmann Witte), 48 (Pcmi), 50 (zentilia), 55 (Nik Frey), 58 (Darren Baker), 60 (Michael Shake), 64 (James Steidl), 66 (Feng Yu), 67 (Theresa Martinez), 70 (Benicce), 72 (senicphoto), 76 (Robert Mizerek), 83 (Liv Friis-larsen), 86 (Vally), 90 (phototom), 93 (Donald Joski), 99 (pat fauve), 102 (Miyazawa), 112 (endostock), 115 (Doreen Salcher), 118 (Yuri Arcurs), 123 (Timon Romeijn), 128 (pressmaster), 132 (Yuri Arcurs), 135 (Andres Rodriguez), 139 (deanm1974), 140 (Jan Schuler), 143 (pressmaster), 145 (Darren Baker), 152 (Nathalie P), 158 (pressmaster)
Gruner+Jahr AG & Co KG/Geo: S. 98
Mc Vitie's: S. 95
MEV: S. 17, 18, 43, 44, 87, 100, 102, 105, 109, 114, 120, 139, 143, 147
picture-alliance/dpa: S. 87
Steffi Becker/BV-1: S. 53, 72, 76, 78, 110, 131